NEGOTIATION AND LAWYERS

Art Hinshaw

John J. Bouma Fellow in Alternative Dispute Resolution
Clinical Professor of Law and Founding Director, Lodestar Dispute Resolution Center
Sandra Day O'Connor College of Law, Arizona State University

Alyson Carrel

Clinical Associate Professor of Law and Co-Director, Center on Negotiation and Mediation
Northwestern University Pritzker School of Law

Leonard L. Riskin

Visiting Professor of Law and Distinguished Senior Fellow, Center on Negotiation and Mediation,
Northwestern University Pritzker School of Law
Chesterfield Smith Professor of Law Emeritus
University of Florida Levin College of Law

Chris Guthrie

Dean and John Wade-Kent Syverud Professor of Law
Vanderbilt University Law School

Richard C. Reuben

James Lewis Parks Professor of Law and Journalism
University of Missouri School of Law

Jennifer K. Robbennolt

Alice Curtis Campbell Professor of Law and Professor of Psychology
University of Illinois College of Law

Nancy A. Welsh

Professor of Law and Director, Dispute Resolution Program
Texas A&M University School of Law

WEST
ACADEMIC
PUBLISHING

© 2021 LEG, Inc. d/b/a West Academic
    444 Cedar Street, Suite 700
    St. Paul, MN 55101
    1-877-888-1330

West, West Academic Publishing, and West Academic are trademarks of West Publishing Corporation, used under license.

Printed in the United States of America

ISBN: 978-1-64708-340-3

ACKNOWLEDGMENTS

Negotiation and Lawyers would not have been possible without the support of the following individuals who provided invaluable research assistance: Rebekah Gordon, Julia Nagle, and Lisa Winkler (Northwestern), as well as McCall Hoerz (Arizona State). We also appreciate the support from our editor at West Academic, Jon Harkness, who shared in our enthusiasm from the beginning of its conception. We all want to thank our co-authors for their time and energy on this book and on *Dispute Resolution and Lawyers*, which paved the way to make *Negotiation and Lawyers* possible.

Last, we gratefully acknowledge the permission extended to reprint excerpts from the works listed below:

Charles B. Craver, Skills and Values: Legal Negotiating, 31, 46–47 (2nd ed. 2012).

Charles B. Craver, The Impact of Negotiator Styles on Bargaining Interactions 35 Am. J. Trial Advoc. 1, 10–13, 17 (2011).

Jayne Seminare Docherty, Culture and Negotiation: Symmetrical Anthropology for Negotiators, 87 Marq. L. Rev. 711, 712–17 (2004).

Noam Ebner, Negotiating via Email, in The Negotiator's Desk Reference 116, 119–129 (Andrea Kupfer Schneider & Christopher Honeyman eds., 2017). Republished with permission of Dispute Resolution Institute.

Noam Ebner, Negotiating via Videoconferencing, in The Negotiator's Desk Reference155, 164–66 (Andrea Kupfer Schneider & Christopher Honeyman eds., 2017). Republished with permission of Dispute Resolution Institute.

Excerpts from GETTING TO YES 2/e by Roger Fisher, William Ury and Bruce Patton. Copyright © 1981, 1991 by Roger Fisher and William Ury. Reprinted by permission of Houghton Mifflin Harcourt Publishing Company. All rights reserved.

Gary Goodpaster, A Primer on the Competitive Bargaining, 1996 J. Disp. Resol. 325, 342–43.

Michael Green, Negotiating while Black, in The Negotiator's Desk Reference 563, 563–581 (Andrea Kupfer Schneider & Christopher Honeyman eds., 2017). Republished with permission of Dispute Resolution Institute.

Art Hinshaw & Jess Alberts, Doing the Right Thing: An Empirical Study of Attorney Negotiation Ethics 16 Harv. Neg. L. Rev. 95, 102–106 (2011). Reprinted with Permission of Harvard University/Law School; permission conveyed through Copyright Clearance Center, Inc.

Russell Korobkin, A Positive Theory of Legal Negotiation, 88 Geo. L.J. 1789, 1792–94 (2000).

Carrie Menkel-Meadow, What Difference Does "Gender Difference" Make? 18 Dispute Resolution Mag. 4, 5–7 (2012). © 2012 by the American Bar Association. Reprinted with permission. All rights reserved. This information or any or portion thereof may not be copied or disseminated in any form or by any means or stored in an electronic database or retrieval system without the express written consent of the American Bar Association.

Carrie Menkel-Meadow, Aha? Is Creativity Possible in Legal Problem Solving and Teachable in Legal Education? 6 Harv. Negot. L. Rev. 97, 105–06, 109–11 (2001). Reprinted with Permission of Harvard University/Law School; permission conveyed through Copyright Clearance Center, Inc.

Carrie Menkel-Meadow, Know When to Show Your Hand, 10 Negot. J. 1, 1–3 (June 2007). Republished with permission of John Wiley and Sons, Inc.; permission conveyed through Copyright Clearance Center, Inc.

Carrie Menkel-Meadow, Toward Another View of Legal Negotiation: The Structure of Problem Solving, 31 U.C.L.A. L. Rev. 754, 755–61, 795–801 (1984).

Beyond Winning: Negotiating to Create Value in Deals and Disputes by Robert H. Mnookin, Scott Peppet and Andrew S. Tulumello, Cambridge, Mass.: The Belknap Press of Harvard University Press, Copyright © 2000 by the President and Fellows of Harvard College.

Leonard Riskin, Further Beyond Reason: Emotions, the Core Concerns, and Mindfulness in Negotiation, 10 Nev. L.J. 289 (2010).

Jennifer K. Robbennolt, Apology-Help or Hindrance? An Empirical Analysis of Apologies' Influence on Settlement Decision making, Dispute Resolution Magazine, Vol 10, Issue 3, 2004. © 2004 by the American Bar Association. Reprinted with permission. All rights reserved. This information or any or portion thereof may not be copied or disseminated in any form or by any means or stored in an electronic database or retrieval system without the express written consent of the American Bar Association.

Andrea K. Schneider, Teaching a New Negotiation Skills Paradigm, 39 Wash. U.J.L. & Pol'y 13, 27–37 (2012).

James K. Sebenius, Negotiation Analysis: A Characterization and Review 38 Management Science 18, 28–30 (Jan 1992). Republished with permission of The Institute for Operations Research and the Management Sciences (INFORMS); permission conveyed through Copyright Clearance Center, Inc.

Excerpt(s) from BARGAINING FOR ADVANTAGE: NEGOTIATION STRATEGIES FOR REASONABLE PEOPLE by G. Richard Shell, copyright © 1999, 2006 by G. Richard Shell. Used by permission of Viking Books, an imprint of Penguin Publishing Group, a division of Penguin Random House LLC. All rights reserved.

Nancy A. Welsh, The Reputational Advantages of Demonstrating Trustworthiness: Using the Reputation Index with Law Students 28 Negot. Journal 117, 136–139 (2011). Republished with permission of John Wiley and Sons, Inc.; permission conveyed through Copyright Clearance Center, Inc.

James E. Westbrook, How to Negotiate With a Jerk Without Being One 1992 J. Disp. Resol. 443, 444–46.

James White, Machiavelli and the Bar: Ethical Limitations on Lying in Negotiation 1980 Am. B. Found. Res. J. 926, 927–29, 931–35. © 1980 by the American Bar Association. Reprinted with permission. All rights reserved. This information or any or portion thereof may not be copied or disseminated in any form or by any means or stored in an electronic database or retrieval system without the express written consent of the American Bar Association.

A.H.

A.C.

L.L.R.

C.G.

R.C.R.

J.K.R.

N.A.W.

TABLE OF CONTENTS

NEGOTIATION AND LAWYERS

INTRODUCTION

Negotiation is an interpersonal process through which we arrange with others to resolve disputes or plan transactions, often by reconciling conflicting, or apparently conflicting, interests. It involves communication, using words or actions, of demands, wishes, and perspectives.

Most lawyers spend a major part of their professional lives engaged in this process. Lawyers in every practice area engage in negotiations, usually with other lawyers. In addition, negotiation makes up an important part of other dispute resolution processes, such as mediation. So many cases in litigation are actually settled through negotiation that Professor Marc Galanter finds it useful to consider the two processes as one "litigotiation" process. Marc Galanter, *World of Deals: Using Negotiation to Teach About Legal Process*, 34 J. Legal Educ. 268, 268 (1984). Professor Gary Goodpaster has gone a step further and suggested that we could learn much by looking at litigation as part of the negotiation process, and Professor J. Maria Glover has gone so far as to suggest that we change the name "Federal Rules of Civil Procedure" to "Federal Rules of Civil Settlement." *See* Gary Goodpaster, *Lawsuits as Negotiations*, 8 Negot. J. 221 (1992); J. Maria Glover, *The Federal Rules of Civil Settlement*, 87 N.Y.U. L. Rev. 1713 (2012).

> **Negotiation Nugget**
>
> In the early 1990s the American Bar Association commissioned a blue ribbon task force, in part, to help develop a curriculum of skills training for law schools. Not surprisingly, the task force identified negotiation as a fundamental legal skill. For more, see Legal Education and Professional Development— An Education Continuum (1992), commonly known as the McCrate Report. https://perma.cc/M4TK-6BLN.

Lawyers do not merely negotiate with other lawyers, however. In their professional lives, lawyers also negotiate with their bosses, partners, subordinates, and with providers of supplies and services. Lawyers also spend a significant portion of their professional lives negotiating with their clients about various aspects of their representation. And in their personal lives, lawyers, like all people, negotiate constantly—with their family, friends, physicians, clergy, and so on.

Because negotiation takes place in such a wide variety of situations, and relies significantly on intuition and judgment, some argue that negotiation skills cannot be taught. We believe, however, that anyone can improve his or her negotiating skills by learning from experience and by practicing, drawing on the social science of negotiation, planning, and reflecting on negotiation.

In this book, we cannot hope to cover the many situations in which lawyers negotiate. For that reason, we attempt to deal with the basics: a set of concepts and suggestions that will help you understand the various negotiation situations in which you may find yourself. In Chapter 1, we begin by focusing on individual characteristics and skills of negotiators. In Chapter 2, we introduce fundamental negotiation concepts that impact negotiation, including the negotiator's dilemma—the push and pull between dividing resources and exploring the underlying interests at the core of the dispute to discover more (or different) resources to divide. Believing that nothing is more practical than a good theory, we hope that this section will give you a solid underpinning for understanding the approaches that you and your counterparts employ in negotiations. Then, in Chapter 3, we explore the negotiation process and the various tasks that good negotiators engage in when negotiating. In Chapter 4, we turn our attention to issues of agency and authority in negotiation, exploring the roles of lawyers and clients. Chapter 5 focuses on the limits on negotiation behavior. In Chapter 6, we examine the potential impacts of culture, gender, and race on the negotiation process. And in Chapter 7, we discuss the increasing impact technology has on negotiation.

CHAPTER 1

OVERVIEW

When negotiating, whether professionally or personally, we regularly rely on our intuition and judgment, factors that are influenced by our life experiences. Some of these experiences influence how we act and react to the situations we find ourselves in, as well as how others react to us. Understanding that negotiation is an interpersonal process, the best way to begin exploring this topic is by thinking and learning about our strengths, our weaknesses, and how others perceive us. Without this understanding, it is all but impossible to become better negotiators.

A.   APPROACH TO CONFLICT

Because negotiation always involves some sort of conflict, be it large or small, a negotiator's general tendencies in responding to conflict and disputes represent a critically important component of negotiation. Professor G. Richard Shell provides the following thought experiment to help negotiators discern which of five approaches to conflict most fit them.

G. RICHARD SHELL, BARGAINING FOR ADVANTAGE: NEGOTIATION STRATEGIES FOR REASONABLE PEOPLE
8–12 (2d ed. 2006)

Your personal negotiation style is a critical variable in bargaining. If you don't know what your instincts and intuitions will tell you to do under different conditions, you will have a great deal of trouble planning effective strategies and responses.

* * *

To begin our exploration of your bargaining strengths, try the following thought experiment. Imagine you are one of ten people, all of whom are strangers, sitting at a big round table in a conference room. Someone comes into the room and makes the following offer: "I will give a prize of one thousand dollars to each of the first two people who can persuade the person sitting opposite to get up, come around the table, and stand behind his or her chair."

Do you have that picture in mind? You are one of ten strangers at the table. You can see the person sitting opposite you, and that person is looking at you. The first two people who can persuade the person sitting opposite to get up, come around the table, and stand behind his or her chair gets $1,000. Everyone else gets nothing.

What strategy would you use to respond to this strange offer? You will need to move quickly because everyone else is also thinking about what to do.

Before reading on, close your eyes and think of your response. Note what strategy comes to your mind first and write it down. Then see what other responses you can think of. The possibilities will help me introduce five generic negotiating strategies, which will, in turn, lead us to a deeper look at your personality as a negotiation variable.

One reaction is to sit tight and do nothing, suspecting a trick or worrying that you might look like a fool running around a table in response to a stranger's offer. "I don't like to negotiate, so I don't do it unless I have to," you might say. This is the avoiding response . . . . Some people might say that avoiding a negotiation is a cop-out, not a bargaining strategy. But you do not have to look very far to notice that many important negotiations are marked by one side or the other studiously avoiding coming to the table. The North Koreans successfully avoided negotiating over their nuclear weapons programs for years—and built up bargaining leverage in the meantime. Presidential candidates in the United States who find themselves ahead in the polls frequently decline to negotiate when their opponents want to increase the number of presidential debates. In general, avoiding is a good strategy when you are happy with the status quo—but it may not be the best approach to the table problem.

Perhaps the most obvious response is to offer the person sitting opposite you $500 if he or she will race around and stand behind your chair. This is the compromise solution. Each person agrees to share the gains equally between them. Compromise is a simple, fair, fast strategy that resolves many negotiations amicably. But is it a good strategy for the table problem? You and your partner may arrive at a quick agreement to split the money evenly, but which of you should run and who should sit? During the few seconds it takes to address this issue, other people are already racing around the table. There is no compromise solution to the question of which of you should run—so a simple compromise does not fully solve the problem. An additional strategy is needed.

That strategy is our third candidate—accommodation. You could simply get up and run behind your opponent's chair. If you do this in response to your partner's offer to split the money, you can refer to that promise as a bargaining standard in any subsequent negotiation over the money. But there may be no money to split. The people who implemented the 100 percent accommodating strategy took off as soon as they heard the stranger's offer and got to their partners' chairs before you did. But they face a problem, too. The lucky people who were the beneficiaries of the accommodating strategy now have $1,000 and the people who ran have nothing. These helpful negotiators must trust the people for whom they earned the money to share it—without the benefit of a prior commitment on how it will be shared. And remember—everyone at the table is a stranger who never expects to see their counterpart again.

The fourth response embodies the competitive strategy. The idea here is to obtain the entire $1,000 as well as the power to decide how it will be shared. One way might be to offer to split the money 50–50 and then later refuse to do so—to renege on your promise. That would obviously be unethical, but some people might do it. After all, there was no mention of a court system to litigate disputes about who said what. An even more aggressive stance would be to lie and say you have a broken leg so you can't move, begging your partner to run as quickly as possible. Are all competitive strategies as ethically dubious as these two? No. We will see examples of many competitive strategies in the pages ahead that are perfectly ethical under any system of morals. But the table problem is not structured well for a strategy that is both ethical and competitive. Moreover, this strategy, like the compromise approach, may take too long to implement.

The final strategy is the most imaginative, given the terms of the offer. You get out of your chair, start running, and scream: "Let's both get behind each other's chairs! We can each make a thousand dollars!" This can work— if you are quick enough. This is the collaborative or problem-solving strategy. Instead of trying to figure out how to divide $1,000 two ways, the person using this approach has the insight to see that there is a way for both parties to get $1,000 out of the situation.

The collaborative strategy is often the hardest to implement. It seeks to discover the underlying problem through good analysis and candid disclosure of interests, find the most elegant solution by brainstorming many options, and resolve tough issues using fair standards and criteria. In many ways, it represents an ideal. As we shall see, problem-solving strategies are especially useful in complex negotiations, such as those faced by international diplomats or corporate negotiators doing mergers or acquisitions. They can also play a useful role in family negotiations, where it is vitally important to avoid having "winners" and "losers." But many obstacles stand in the way of collaborative approaches, such as lack of trust between the parties, greed, personality, cultural differences, and simple lack of imagination.

* * *

Your personal bargaining styles are nothing more (or less) than your inclinations or predispositions to make certain moves when you are negotiating. These inclinations can come from many sources—childhood, family, early professional experiences, mentors, ethical systems or beliefs, and so on. And your inclinations can change over time as your knowledge of negotiation grows and you gain more confidence in a wider range of skills. But I genuinely believe that most of us have a set of core personality traits that make radical changes in our basic bargaining preferences difficult.

POINTS FOR DISCUSSION

1.   What is your most likely response to conflict? Your least likely response? Learning about the various responses to conflict and their own tendencies provides negotiators with a general framework for understanding themselves and their counterparts, and for making sense of their interactions.

2.   What do you think happens when two negotiators using the "competing" approach negotiate with one another? Two negotiators using the "avoiding" approach? Two negotiators using the "compromising" approach? How about a "competing" negotiator and an "accommodating" negotiator? A "competing" negotiator and an "avoiding" negotiator?

> **Negotiation Nugget**
>
> There are a number of online tools one can use to learn how you respond to conflict. One of the most recognized and used is the *Thomas-Kilmann Conflict Mode* Instrument. The categories Shell discusses in this excerpt are identified there.

3.   Do you think you respond in the same manner in professional settings as in personal settings? Is your natural response the same when you are negotiating on your own behalf as when you are negotiating for someone else? What other contextual factors might—or should—influence your response to conflict? When Dean Jennifer Gerarda Brown asks her students to complete the Thomas-Kilmann Instrument to test conflict styles, she instructs them to think in terms of the relationship in which they can be their " 'truest self' . . . in which you do not assume an artificial persona specific to the relationship." She then reminds them that the response demanded by

their role—e.g., representing a client in a legal negotiation—"may be a departure from what they identified as authentic, instinctive, or reflexive." Jennifer Gerarda Brown, *Empowering Students to Create and Claim Value Through the Thomas-Kilmann Conflict Mode Instrument*, 28 Neg. J. 79, 84–85 (2012). Professor Leonard Riskin provides additional insights into the differences between our negotiation styles in professional settings versus personal settings by combining conflict resolution theories with a model of the mind called Internal Family Systems (IFS). The IFS model provides a construct for understanding why our "truest self" may not always present itself depending on the context of the negotiation. Leonard R. Riskin, *Managing Inner and Outer Conflict: Selves, Subpersonalities, and Internal Family Systems*, 18 Harv. Negot. L. Rev. 1 (2013).

4.   Professor Leonard Riskin has also argued that negotiators who practice mindfulness meditation are likely to gain insight into their own personalities, moods, and the way they respond to conflict and, consequently, perform better in negotiations. See Leonard L. Riskin, *The Contemplative Lawyer: On the Potential Contributions of Mindfulness Meditation to Law Students, Lawyers, and Their Clients*, 7 Harv. Negot. L. Rev. 1 (2002).

B.   NEGOTIATION SKILLS

When speaking of negotiation skills, the question naturally arises— exactly what skills are we talking about? You may be thinking of skills like listening, asking questions, and other discrete skills. Professor Andrea Schneider has analyzed the skills negotiators employ to identify several meta-skills, drawn primarily from the approaches to conflict discussion earlier in this chapter, to help place many negotiation concepts in context.

ANDREA KUPFER SCHNEIDER, TEACHING A NEW NEGOTIATION SKILLS PARADIGM
39 Wash. U.J.L. & Pol'y 13, 27–37 (2012)

A.   Effective Skills Permit Stylistic Choices

[W]ith more skills in their toolbox, students will best be able to prepare, start, respond, and conclude negotiations in a more thoughtful manner. . . . In thinking about what makes any given skill more effective, . . . I've organized our skill expectations along a spectrum of minimal to average skill level to best practices.

1.   Assertiveness

The ability to assert yourself in a negotiation can depend on your alternatives, your goals, your research or knowledge in the area, and your ability to speak persuasively. In order to assert oneself, a minimal skill might be some level of competence and knowledge. An average skill would be to have fully researched the situation and be well-prepared. Best practices would include confidence based on competence and knowledge.

. . . Minimal skill in speaking would be the ability to explain your client's position. Average skill would include speaking clearly about why this position is worthwhile. Best practices would include researching in advance what types of arguments, criteria (legal precedent, industry practice, etc.), and salesmanship techniques work best with your particular counterpart. There are, no doubt, other skills as part of assertiveness that could be similarly mapped.

2.   Empathy

Empathy is linked to success in a variety of careers. The skill of "empathic accuracy," according to William Ickes, is what creates "the most tactful advisors, the most diplomatic officials, [and] the most effective negotiators." Even lawyers and economists now recognize that separating decision-making from emotions is detrimental.

> **Note**
>
> Interests are the underlying motivations driving an individual's demands. This concept is explored in more depth in Chapter 2.

Being empathetic in a negotiation requires a complex mix of skills—a willingness to hear the other side, open-mindedness or curiosity, good questioning and excellent listening, among others. First, one needs the belief and understanding that your counterpart might have something to contribute. And so a minimal skill would be to distinguish between the rare win-lose negotiations and those that might have room for joint gain. An average skill would be the ability to find integrative potential. Best practices would be to translate the parties' interests into realistic integrative proposals.

Second, one needs the skills to gather information about one's counterpart to build the relationship in order to work together substantively. A minimal skill might be to ask questions of the other side in order to get information about them to help move the process along. An average skill would perhaps be to ask questions to uncover the counterpart's interests and needs. Best practices would include having a learning conversation in order to better understand the counterpart's client and that client's situation in order to propose solutions that respond to those needs.

Similarly, a minimal skill in listening would be to let the other side explain their case without interrupting. An average skill would be to ask questions when they are done to both clarify and demonstrate one's listening. Best practices would include looping or active listening to confirm that you accurately understand their perspective and that, even if you don't agree with their position, you respect their position.

3. Flexibility

Talented negotiators work to find a variety of ways to get the job done both in their strategic choices as well as more flexible outcomes. Being flexible in negotiation allows a stylistic move from simple compromising to more sophisticated integrative solutions. It also helps to prevent stalemate. And so a minimal skill on flexible strategic choices might be choosing a style based on a particular context or counterpart. An average skill would be shifting your strategy or tactics in the course of the negotiation to respond to your counterpart. Best practices would include careful thinking about the reputation of your counterpart, selecting skills on that basis as well as your own skill set and your client's situation, and then adapting your skills as needed based on your counterpart and newly acquired information in the course of the negotiation.

In terms of finding creative outcomes, Leigh Thompson writes about three types of creativity: fluency (the ability to create many solutions); flexibility (the ability to generate different solutions); and originality (the ability to come up with a unique solution). A negotiator will want to work on all three of types in order to be most effective and to think about the processes (for example, brainstorming) that might assist in creating different solutions. A minimal skill would be simply knowing your priorities so that you could do trade-offs at the table. An average skill could be preparing one or two different tradeoffs that might work (cash payment in exchange for earlier settlement, length of contract in exchange for lower salary, etc.) Best practices would be to examine a variety of creative processes both before and during a negotiation—non-specific compensation, contingent agreements, adding issues, etc.—that could provide additional solutions.

4. Social Intuition

We know that having a pleasant and welcoming personality helps effectiveness [sic] in life. The work of Daniel Goleman on emotional and social intelligence has made it clear that successful people manage their emotions and social skills in order to get along with others. . . . Goleman outlines the significant business and life advantages to being more socially intelligent. And recent articles have focused on the importance of teaching these skills to lawyers.

Social intelligence itself is defined as both social awareness (much of this falls under empathy discussed above) and social facility, which includes interacting and presenting ourselves to others. Others have also written about the importance of being nice and of the "No-Asshole" rule in business as being exceedingly successful.

> **Negotiation Nugget**
>
> Daniel Goleman has written several books on emotional intelligence that are widely available in libraries, bookstores, and online.

In a more specific negotiation context, we have seen this from several angles. The research on tone in negotiation shows that positive moods can make people more creative and more likely to use integrative strategies. The converse is also true— negotiators in bad moods are more likely to be competitive.

Similarly, in rating negotiators as effective, [the results of a prior study] show how many adjectives covering social skills fit into effectiveness: personable, rational, perceptive, self-controlled, sociable, helpful, smooth, etc. Unsurprisingly, these adjectives could be mapped onto a measure of social intelligence.

* * *

In terms of setting rapport, for example, Leigh Thompson suggests that a "[s]avvy negotiator[] increase[s her] effectiveness by making themselves familiar to the other party." A minimal skill would be to have a level of cordiality. An average skill level would be to schmooze with the other side, asking questions about them, and breaking the ice. Best practices would include advance research to find areas of commonality and to be genuinely friendly and curious.

5.   Ethicality

Perceptions of a negotiator's ethicality—his trustworthiness and willingness to follow the ethical rules—has a direct impact on reputation. And reputation—the perception of ethicality—is directly linked to effectiveness in negotiation. A minimal level of skill would be to follow the professional rules of responsibility and not actively deceive the other side. An average level of skill would be to also view possible deceptive behavior through the lens of likely ramifications including your reputation. Best practices would include being actually trustworthy and treating the other side fairly.

* * *

Being both trustworthy and trustful includes defending yourself against the unethical. A minimal level of skill would be to assume that others might lie to you and contemplate what you can do about that. An average level of skill would include asking defensive questions to double check their assertions and writing compliance measures into the contract. Best practices could include building a sufficiently strong relationship so that it is more difficult for others to lie to you.

6.   Putting the Skills Together

Ideally, we could create a three dimensional figure that demonstrates how all these skills relate to one another. A five-sided pyramid in which each skill could be measured would have been lovely. If one imagines, however, that the pyramid has been unfolded, it might look something like this:

Negotiation Origami

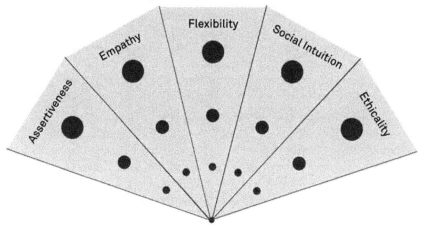

● Best practice

● Average practice

• Minimum practice

Each person could measure themselves on each skill independently while working to broaden their skill arsenal. Each skill might not be utilized in each negotiation but the skill-set itself would always be available.

POINTS FOR DISCUSSION

1.   Some might argue that some of the skills that Professor Schneider identifies are more a function of personality and therefore cannot be taught, especially to adults. Do you agree or disagree with this claim? Might this be the case with some more than others? If so, which ones and why?

Digging Deeper

Note that these skills appear to be interpersonal skills more so than "legal" analytical skills. Why would that be? Is that problematic in any way?

2.   In 2016, the Institute for the Advancement of the American Legal System published a report finding a majority of practicing attorneys value characteristics such as integrity, work ethic, and resilience in recent law school graduates more than legal knowledge and skills. The Institute for the Advancement of the American Legal System, *Foundations of Practice: The Whole Lawyer and the Character Quotient* (2016). How might you gain these types of skills?

3.   Implicit in Professor Schneider's article is the importance of listening, which is often identified as the most essential of all lawyering skills. Poor listening skills means missing out on important data—interests, goals, preferences, constraints, etc.—from clients and counterparts. Listening connotes respect and caring, and people are more likely to trust those who they believe listen to them. According to Professors Jennifer K. Robbennolt and Jean R. Sternlight,

> [I]n order to both listen effectively and appear to be listening effectively, lawyers should typically let their counterpart talk without interruptions. Similarly, it is useful for lawyers to focus on listening to the answers provided rather than to assume that they know what the other will say or be preoccupied with what to say or ask next. A good listener uses follow-up questions to probe for additional details: "Can you tell me a bit more about that?" A good listener also uses follow-up questions to clarify that she has understood what the speaker has said: "So, you've said that . . . Have I got that right?" Such questions indicate to the speaker that the listener has heard him, verify the listener's understanding, and invite any necessary clarification or elaboration. Such active listening motivates speakers to continue.

Jennifer K. Robbennolt & Jean R. Sternlight, PSYCHOLOGY FOR LAWYERS: UNDERSTANDING THE HUMAN FACTORS IN NEGOTIATION, LITIGATION, AND DECISION MAKING 161–63 (2012).

4.   Researchers have found positive correlations among listening and perceptions of trustworthiness, willingness to disclose information, and procedural justice. See Rebecca Hollander-Blumoff & Tom R. Tyler, *Procedural Justice in Negotiation: Procedural Justice, Outcome Fairness, and Integrative Potential*, 33 Law & Soc. Inq. 473 (2008); Rebecca Hollander-Blumoff, *Just Negotiation*, 88 Wash. U. L. Q. 381 (2010). Procedural justice focuses on the fairness of the procedure separate from the fairness of the outcome. Research convincingly demonstrates that if people judge a process to be fair, they are more likely to perceive procedure's outcome to be fair and to comply with the outcome—even if it is unfavorable to them. See E. ALLAN LIND & TOM R. TYLER, THE SOCIAL PSYCHOLOGY OF PROCEDURAL JUSTICE (1988); Nancy A. Welsh, *Making Deals in Court-Connected Mediation: What's Justice Got to Do with It?*, 79 Wash. U. L. Q. 787, 859–61 (2001).

5.   Relatively straightforward paraphrasing can be effective as a means to demonstrate understanding of key content. But *reflective* or *active listening* is an especially effective device for conveying non-judgmental empathetic understanding, developing trust, and eliciting additional information. In active listening, the interviewer restates both the content and the feelings she believes are associated with the statement as explained below.

> Active listening is a particular form of listening that involves conveying to the speaker . . . that you have heard both the substance of what she has said as well as its emotional content. You do this by "mirroring" or paraphrasing what you have heard said explicitly, and by putting into words the implicit feelings emanating from the speaker; sometimes you may answer on only one of these levels (addressing explicit content or implicit feelings, but not both), but often you will need to respond both to the [words and] emotions.

Robert Dinerstein, Stephen Ellman, Isabelle Gunning & Ann Shalleck, *Connection, Capacity and Morality in Lawyer-Client Relationships*, 10 Clinical L. Rev. 755, 758–62 (2004).

6.   Active listening may seem a little contrived when you first try it. But with practice it can quickly become much more natural as you adapt the principles to your own style and personality. But it does take practice. To practice the listening concepts addressed in this chapter, choose a classmate or friend and spend ten minutes actively listening to him as he describes a dispute in which he was involved. Then let him actively listen to you as you spend ten minutes describing a dispute in which you were involved. Was active listening easy or difficult? To the extent it was difficult, what made it difficult? How was it different from a normal conversation, or a more formal interview? Did you feel that your counterpart really understood the facts involved in your dispute? Did you feel that your counterpart really understood how you felt about the dispute?

7.   Another way to practice active listening is to try it the next time you have a relatively minor dispute, disagreement, or conflict with someone where you get the sense that the two of you are just talking past each other. At that point, make a conscious effort to try it and see how it goes.

8.   Active listening is an important technique for improving our listening skills, but it is not the only one. One more technique that can be very helpful is the Loop of Understanding, commonly called "looping." Although the technique is similar to and borrows much from the active listening method discussed above, looping extends it much further. In active listening, we reflect back to the speaker our sense of what they were saying in terms of both the facts and the speaker's emotional sense of the experience. The loop of understanding takes the additional step of having the speaker confirm or correct the listener's understanding. There are four steps to the process:

1.   The speaker says what he or she is going to say.

2.   The listener reflects back what he or she understood, both the facts and emotional content. (This is essentially active listening.)

3.   The listener then seeks confirmation from the speaker that the listener fully understood the speaker.

4.   The speaker confirms the accuracy of the listener's understanding or corrects it by providing more information and beginning the loop again (steps 1–3). This loop continues until the speaker is fully satisfied that the listener completely understands the listener.

9.   Critically, looping also *communicates to the speaker* that the listener actually understands what the speaker said and how the speaker felt about it. This demonstration of understanding eliminates doubt in the mind of the speaker and allows for a deeper connection between the speaker and the listener. Similarly, it allows the speaker to correct the listener if the listener is wrong, and to do so by focusing precisely on the point of misunderstanding. Interestingly, it can also clarify and deepen the speaker's own thoughts in that the listener may have accurately reflected back what the speaker was communicating, only for the speaker to find that there was more to it than he or she thought, factually, emotionally, or both. See ROBERT MNOOKIN, SCOTT PEPPET & ANDREW S. TULUMELLO, BEYOND WINNING: NEGOTIATING TO CREATE VALUE IN DEALS AND DISPUTES 64–65 (2000).

CHAPTER 2

FUNDAMENTAL CONCEPTS

In 1959, then-President Dwight D. Eisenhower gave a televised address in which he reflected on a recently completed European trip and explained his decision to invite the then-leader of the Soviet Union to the United States during the middle of the Cold War. His hope was to reduce tensions between the countries through negotiation, and he explained his negotiation philosophy as follows: "fundamentals, with flexibility in tactics and method, is the key to any hope of progress in negotiation." *Text of Eisenhower Speech on His European Trip*, N.Y. TIMES,

Negotiation Nugget

To read this interesting speech in its entirety, go to https://www. presidency.ucsb.edu/documents/ radio-and-television-report-the- american-people-the-european-trip.

Sept. 11, 1959, at 8. Although he was speaking in the context of international relations, we believe this philosophy applies to all negotiation contexts.

No matter whether you are experienced or inexperienced, becoming a better negotiator requires a firm understanding of fundamental negotiation concepts. These foundational concepts—interests, objective criteria, the best alternative to a negotiated agreement (BATNA), the negotiator's dilemma, and reputation—guide negotiators' preparation, strategy decisions, and the success or failure of both the negotiation itself and the implementation of the negotiated outcome.

A. INTERESTS

Understanding the difference between interests and positions is the most fundamental skill a negotiator can learn. A position is what someone says she wants or is entitled to have. For instance, a plaintiff in a personal injury case who asks for money damages of $50,000 is asserting a position. An interest is the need or motive that underlies that position. The plaintiff might be motivated by interests in paying bills, being treated with respect, clarifying her relationship with the defendant, receiving an apology, or punishing the defendant. Money damages in a particular amount may or may not satisfy each of these interests. Negotiations can focus on positions, interests, or both. In this excerpt, Professor Roger Fisher and Messrs. William Ury and Bruce Patton explain the concept of interests in negotiation in detail.

ROGER FISHER, WILLIAM URY & BRUCE PATTON, GETTING TO YES: NEGOTIATING AGREEMENT WITHOUT GIVING IN
42–46 (3d ed. 2011)

Negotiation Nugget

Mary Parker Follett (1868–1933) was a pioneer in the field of management and organizational behavior. She believed that conflict created opportunities for inventive solutions that became better known as the phrase "win-win" negotiations.

Consider Mary Parker Follett's story of two men quarreling in a library. One wants the window open and the other wants it closed. They bicker back and forth about how much to leave it open: a crack, halfway, three-quarters of the way. No solution satisfies them both. Enter the librarian. She asks one why he wants the window open: "To get some fresh air." She asks the other why he wants it closed: "To avoid the draft." After thinking a minute, she opens wide a window in the next room, bringing in fresh air without a draft.

For a wise solution reconcile interests, not positions

This story is typical of many negotiations. Since the parties' problem appears to be a conflict of positions, and since their goal is to agree on a position, they naturally tend to think and talk about positions—and in the process often reach an impasse. The librarian could not have invented the solution she did if she had focused only on the two men's stated positions of wanting the window open or closed. Instead she looked to their underlying interests of fresh air and no draft. This difference between positions and interests is crucial.

Interests define the problem. The basic problem in a negotiation lies not in conflicting positions, but in the conflict between each side's needs, desires, concerns, and fears.

The parties may say: "I am trying to get him to stop that real estate development next door." Or "We disagree. He wants $300,000 for the house. I won't pay a penny more than $250,000." But on a more basic level the problem is: "He needs the cash; I want peace and quiet." Or "He needs at least $300,000 to pay off the mortgage and put 20 percent down on his new house. I told my family that I wouldn't pay more than $250,000 for a house."

Such desires and concerns are interests. Interests motivate people; they are the silent movers behind the hubbub of positions. Your position is something you have decided upon. Your interests are what caused you to so decide.

* * *

Reconciling interests rather than positions works for two reasons. First, for every interest there usually exist several possible positions that could satisfy it. All too often people simply adopt the most obvious position . . . . When you do look behind opposed positions for the motivating interests, you can often find an alternative position that meets not only your interests but theirs as well. . . .

Reconciling interests rather than compromising between positions also works because behind opposed positions lie many more interests than conflicting ones.

Behind opposed positions lie shared and compatible interests, as well as conflicting ones. We tend to assume that because the other side's positions are opposed to ours, their interests must also be opposed. If we have an interest in defending ourselves, then they must want to attack us. If we have an interest in minimizing the rent, then their interest must be to maximize it. In many negotiations, however, a close examination of the underlying interests will reveal the existence of many more interests that are shared or compatible than ones that are opposed.

For example, look at the interests a tenant shares with a prospective landlord:

1. Both want stability. The landlord wants a stable tenant; the tenant wants a permanent address.

2. Both would like to see the apartment well maintained. The tenant is going to live there; the landlord wants to increase the value of the apartment as well as the reputation of the building.

3. Both are interested in a good relationship with each other. The landlord wants a tenant who pays the rent regularly; the tenant wants a responsive landlord who will carry out the necessary repairs.

They may also have interests that do not conflict but simply differ. For example:

1. The tenant may not want to deal with fresh paint, to which he is allergic. The landlord will not want to pay the costs of repainting all the other apartments.

2. The landlord would like the security of a down payment of the first month's rent, and he may want it by tomorrow. The tenant, knowing that this is a good apartment, may be indifferent on the question of paying tomorrow or later.

When weighed against these shared and divergent interests, the opposed interests in minimizing the rent and maximizing the return seem more manageable. The shared interests will likely result in a long lease, an agreement to share the cost of improving the apartment, and efforts by both parties to accommodate each other in the interest of a good relationship. The divergent interests may perhaps be reconciled by a down payment tomorrow and an agreement by the landlord to paint the apartment provided the tenant buys the paint. The precise amount of the rent is all that remains to be settled, and the market for rental apartments may define that fairly well.

Agreement is often made possible precisely because interests differ. You and a shoe-seller may both like money and shoes. Relatively, his interest in the fifty dollars exceeds his interest in a pair of shoes. For you, the situation is reversed: you like the shoes better than the fifty dollars. Hence the deal. Shared interests and differing but complementary interests can both serve as the building blocks for a wise agreement.

How do you identify interests? The benefit of looking behind positions for interests is clear. How to go about it is less clear. A position is likely to be concrete and explicit; the interests underlying it may well be unexpressed, intangible, and perhaps inconsistent. How do you go about understanding the interests involved in a negotiation, remembering that figuring out *their* interests will be at least as important as figuring out *yours*?

Ask "Why?" One basic technique is to put yourself in their shoes. Examine each position they take, and ask yourself "Why?" Why, for instance, does your landlord prefer to fix the rent—in a five-year lease—year by year? The answer you may come up with, to be protected against increasing costs, is probably one of his interests. You can also ask the landlord himself why he takes a particular position. If you do, make clear that you are asking not for justification of this position, but for an understanding of the needs, hopes, fears, or desires that it serves. "What's your basic concern, Mr. Peters, in wanting the lease to run for no more than three years?"

Ask "Why not?" Think about their choice. One of the most useful ways to uncover interests is first to identify the basic decision that those on the other side probably see you asking them for, and then to ask yourself why they have not made that decision. What interests of theirs stand in the way? If you are trying to change their minds, the starting point is to figure out where their minds are now.

POINTS FOR DISCUSSION

1.   Grande Lum, the former Director of the Community Relations Service at the U.S. Department of Justice, describes the difference between interests and positions as follows:

> Interests are the nuts and bolts of agreements. They are the concerns, drivers, incentives, underlying needs, and motivators of the parties. They are the reasons people are involved in a negotiation in the first place. . . .
>
> Interests are not the same as positions. For negotiation purposes, I define positions as the demands of the parties. Another way of explaining the difference between positions and interests is to say that positions are what you want, while interests are what you need.

> **Negotiation Nugget**
>
> Professor Noam Ebner has created a short YouTube video describing the difference between positions and interests that you can watch here: https://www.youtube.com/watch?v=CcW5A1c3-Fc.

GRANDE LUM, THE NEGOTIATION FIELDBOOK: SIMPLE STRATEGIES TO HELP YOU NEGOTIATE EVERYTHING 6 (2d ed. 2011). Even though understanding the difference between positions and interests is easy, it takes practice to get good at recognizing the difference in real negotiations.

2.   Professor Leonard L. Riskin believes that understanding the concept of interests is critical for lawyers. He states: "[T]eaching about interests is my most fundamental goal in nearly every course I teach. I believe strongly that lawyers who understand and attend to interests will serve their clients better." Leonard L. Riskin, *Beginning with Yes: A Review Essay on Michael Wheeler's* The Art of Negotiation: How to Improvise Agreement in a Chaotic World, 16 Cardozo J. Confl. Resol. 605, 617 (2015).

3.   According to Professor Fisher and Mssrs. Ury and Patton the most powerful interests are basic human needs such as security, economic well-being, a sense of belonging, recognition, and control over one's life. They suggest that negotiations will make little progress as long as one side believes that the other is threatening the fulfilment of such basic human needs. Christopher W. Moore has categorized interests into three distinct groups—substantive interests, procedural interests, and psychological interests. Substantive interests are defined as tangible outcomes or benefits that a party wants to have satisfied during the negotiation. Procedural interests are preferences about how the dispute resolution process proceeds. There are two types of psychological interests—how individuals and groups are treated both in the negotiation and outside of it, and how negotiating parties feel about themselves and their counterparts. CHRISTOPHER W. MOORE, THE MEDIATION PROCESS: PRACTICAL STRATEGIES FOR RESOLVING CONFLICT 127–30 (4th ed. 2014).

> **Digging Deeper**
>
> How does this compare with the more recognized Maslow's hierarchy of needs?

4.   Negotiators typically have several competing interests at play during any single negotiation, and these interests may change over time or moment-to-moment. How is it that negotiators should contend with competing and changing interests?

5.   Fully understanding our client's interests can be extremely challenging. What does it take to achieve this task? To the extent that conflict tends to evoke emotions, what impact are such emotions likely to have on our clients' ability to understand and communicate their interests? On lawyers' ability to understand and advance those interests?

6.   The advice to focus on interests assumes that negotiators can identify what it is they want to get out of a negotiation. When asked why they want something, negotiators are expected to know the answer (even if they choose not to disclose it). But is this as easy as it sounds? Research regarding affective forecasting indicates that people can make accurate predictions about their general preferences, but they may miscalculate exactly how happy they will be or how long their happiness will last. This is likely to be particularly true for "one-shot" negotiators. See Chris Guthrie & David F. Sally, *Miswanting, in* THE NEGOTIATOR'S FIELDBOOK: A DESK REFERENCE FOR THE EXPERIENCED NEGOTIATOR 277 (Andrea Kupfer Schneider & Christopher Honeyman eds., 2006). What is a lawyer to do—be true to the client's expressed interests or presume the one-shot client does not really know what she wants? Can a lawyer disregard the client's stated interests?

7.   As part of their preparation strategy, negotiators should also do their best to identify their negotiation counterparts' interests. There may be overlapping, common, or non-competitive interests that can serve as easy ways to create value in the negotiation. Even if the interests are conflicting, understanding them helps negotiators learn what kinds of options and offers may appeal to their counterparts. Seeing a situation from a counterpart's viewpoint is difficult and will involve assumptions and guesswork. Nevertheless, having some initial idea of what may be motivating a negotiation counterpart is critical. According to Professor G. Richard Shell, the best way to think about a counterpart's interests is to ask this question: "How might it serve the other party's interests to help you achieve your goals?" G. RICHARD SHELL, BARGAINING FOR ADVANTAGE: NEGOTIATION STRATEGIES FOR REASONABLE PEOPLE 82 (2d ed. 2006).

Note

In Chapter 3, we detail specific preparation strategies regarding reservation point and goals; options; information gathering; and emotions.

8.   Professor David Matz has identified four reasons why it may be difficult for a negotiator to really "know" the other party's interests:

First, parties have an incentive to lie. As almost all disputes have a significant, often dominant, distributive aspect, parties can rationally conclude that sharing their interests with their negotiating opponent can be detrimental to their cause. This incentive to lie, while often lamented, is well documented. * * *

Second, . . . a further disadvantage in knowing a party's interests [is that a] demand as expressed . . . can "stand for" a variety of interests. Almost all the interests . . . , for example, can be expressed as money. Compounding the difficulty of knowing which interests are "real" is the fact that it is more culturally acceptable to express some interests than others (e.g. money is acceptable, vengeance is not).

Digging Deeper

Is it ethically acceptable, from purely a moral perspective, to lie in negotiation? Why or why not? For a discussion of ethics in negotiation see Chapter 5.

Third, most parties in disputes are not isolated negotiators. They have constituencies, "second tables," organizational contexts, or significant others. Any of these influences may be part of the negotiator's concerns, an audience to which she will later have to appeal. . . . Moreover, if the negotiator is representing an organization, the interests within that group may be unfocused, conflicted, or evolving. The classic line "I'd love to but my boss won't let me," captures the . . . problem well. Is the boss real or a dodge? An interest or a convenience?

The final source of difficulty is the hardest to describe, but it is also perhaps the most important. Conventionally, a party has interests in the same sense that she has car keys: they are objective, discrete things. . . . This picture seems to me inaccurate. The interests of a party are much more like a kaleidoscope than they are like a collection of discrete things. The surface clarity, the publicly stated "position," masks an active fluidity. There are in the kaleidoscope some recognizable elements, but the boundaries among the elements keep shifting. . . .

David E. Matz, *Ignorance and Interests*, 4 Harv. Negot. L. Rev. 59, 63–64 (1999).

B. OBJECTIVE CRITERIA

While interests play a key role in negotiation, objective criteria— independent external standards—typically play a large role in the distributive issues in negotiation. In the following excerpt, Professor G. Richard Shell explains why objective criteria lend an aura of impartiality, legitimacy, and fairness in negotiations.

G. RICHARD SHELL, BARGAINING FOR ADVANTAGE: NEGOTIATION STRATEGIES FOR REASONABLE PEOPLE
43–44 (2d ed. 2006)

Why are standards and norms—particularly standards the other side has adopted—such an important part of bargaining? Because, all else being equal, people like to be seen as consistent and rational in the way they make decisions.

Psychologists have a name for this need-to-appear-reasonable phenomenon. They call it "the consistency principle." Social psychologists have discovered that people have a deep need to avoid the disjointed, erratic, and uncomfortable psychological states that arise when our actions are manifestly inconsistent with previously expressed, long-held, or widely shared standards and beliefs.

Most of us have complex "consistency webs" that are interconnected at many levels of our personality. Because we like to keep these webs intact, we rationalize our actions so they appear (at least in our own eyes) to be consistent with our prior beliefs. We are also more open to persuasion when we see a proposed course of action as being consistent with a course we have already adopted.

Negotiations are fertile ground for observing the consistency principle at work. Whether we are aware of it or not, we sometimes feel a tug to agree with the other party when the standards or norms he or she articulates are consistent with prior statements and positions we ourselves have taken. We also feel uncomfortable (though we may keep this to ourselves) when the other side correctly points out that we have been inconsistent in one of our positions or arguments. In short, standards and norms are—or can be—more than just intellectual pawns in bargaining debates. They can be strong, motivating factors in the way negotiations proceed.

POINTS FOR DISCUSSION

1.   Noting that objective criteria need to be independent, legitimate, and practical, Professor Fisher and Mssrs. Ury and Patton identify several potential sources of objective criteria, including market value, precedent, scientific judgment, professional standards, efficiency, costs, what a court would decide, moral standards, and tradition. ROGER FISHER, WILLIAM URY & BRUCE PATTON, GETTING TO YES: NEGOTIATING AGREEMENT WITHOUT GIVING IN 86 (3d ed. 2011). What other sources of objective criteria can you identify?

2.   Dean Chris Guthrie has described objective criteria as the single most important concept for legal negotiators. Chris Guthrie, *Using Bargaining for Advantage in Law School Negotiation Courses*, 16 Ohio St. J. Disp. Resol. 219, 234 (2000). Why might that be?

3.   According to Director Lum, in conjunction with the subjective nature of interests, objective criteria "help[ ] provide a landscape of possible options and help[ ] identify what range of solutions you can assert." THE NEGOTIATION FIELDBOOK: SIMPLE STRATEGIES TO HELP YOU NEGOTIATE EVERYTHING 24 (2d ed. 2011).

4.   Many negotiators spend a significant amount of time focusing on which standards should form the basis of a deal. Martin E. Latz calls the discussion about which standards should be used "the standards dance." For example, a buyer and seller negotiating the purchase of a house may spend time discussing the house's price based on several standards such as the price per square foot of the house, the house's last selling price and the increase or decrease in value of the housing market since then, or the comparable price of similar houses that have recently sold in the same area. Latz admonishes "that you can't [do the standards] dance well if you don't do your homework." What homework is this? Latz advises negotiators to identify the various standards that they might use during the negotiation and also to identify the standards the other side may want to use. Next, he recommends preparing arguments in favor of the standards you prefer and against the standards you find

disadvantageous. MARTIN E. LATZ, GAIN THE EDGE: NEGOTIATING TO GET WHAT YOU WANT 140–41 (2004).

5.   The authors of *Getting to Yes* add a layer to the standards dance. They argue that, when there is a dispute as to which standard to apply, the negotiators should "look for an objective basis for deciding between them, such as which standard has been used by the parties in the past or which standard is more widely applied." ROGER FISHER, WILLIAM URY & BRUCE PATTON, GETTING TO YES: REACHING AGREEMENT WITHOUT GIVING IN 90 (3d ed. 2011). Is this realistic?

C.   BEST ALTERNATIVE TO A NEGOTIATED AGREEMENT

A negotiator's best alternative to a negotiated agreement (BATNA) is an incredibly useful negotiation concept analyzing what alternatives a negotiator has if they are unable to reach an agreement. BATNAs act as a backstop to keep negotiators from agreeing to deals that they would be better off passing up. The following excerpt addresses in depth how to develop one's BATNA.

ROGER FISHER, WILLIAM URY, AND BRUCE PATTON, GETTING TO YES: NEGOTIATING AGREEMENT WITHOUT GIVING IN
105–06 (3d ed. 2011)

Vigorous exploration of what you will do if you do not reach agreement can greatly strengthen your hand. Attractive alternatives are not just sitting there waiting for you; you usually have to develop them. Generating possible BATNAs requires three distinct operations: (1) inventing a list of actions you might conceivably take if no agreement is reached; (2) improving some of the more promising ideas and converting them into practical alternatives; and (3) selecting, tentatively, the one alternative that seems best.

The first operation is inventing. If by the end of the month Company X does not make you a satisfactory job offer, what are some things you might do? Take a job with Company Y? Look in another city? Start a business on your own? What else? For a labor union, alternatives to a negotiated agreement would presumably include calling a strike, working without a contract, giving a sixty-day notice of a strike, asking for a mediator, and calling on union members to "work to rule."

> **Negotiation Nugget**
>
> A mediator is a neutral 3rd party that facilitates discussion among disputing parties.

The second stage is to improve the best of your ideas and turn the most promising into real alternatives. If you are thinking about working in Chicago, try to turn that idea into at least one job offer there. With a Chicago job offer in hand (or even having discovered that you are unable to produce one) you are much better prepared to assess the merits of a New York offer. While a labor union is still negotiating, it should convert the ideas of calling in a mediator and of striking into drafts of specific operational decisions ready for execution. The union might take a vote of its membership to authorize a strike if settlement is not achieved by the time the contract expires.

The final step in developing a BATNA is selecting the best among the alternatives. If you do not reach agreement in the negotiations, which of your realistic alternatives do you now plan to pursue?

Having gone through this effort, you now have a BATNA. Judge every offer against it. The better your BATNA, the greater your ability to improve the terms of any negotiated agreement. Knowing what you are going to do if the negotiation does not lead to agreement will give you additional confidence in the negotiation process. It is easier to break off negotiations if you know where you're going. The greater your willingness to break off negotiations, the more forcefully you can present your interests and the basis on which you believe an agreement should be reached.

POINTS FOR DISCUSSION

1.   According to Professor Fisher and Mssrs. Ury and Patton, "[BATNA] is the standard against which any proposed agreement should be measured. That is the only standard which can prevent you both from accepting terms that are too unfavorable and rejecting terms it would be in your interest to accept." GETTING TO YES 102 (3d ed. 2011). Thus, if a negotiator's BATNA is more attractive than an offer on the table, the negotiator should reject the offer. In this respect a negotiator's BATNA helps determine her reservation point, the point where a negotiator will refuse an offer and walk away from the deal.

> **Digging Deeper**
>
> What is the difference between one's BATNA and a reservation point, the point where one will not go past?

2. What are the respective BATNAs of the parties to a breach of contract claim in settlement negotiations? Is each party's best alternative simply going to trial? If so, is a BATNA a helpful concept in the litigation context? Does the same apply to plea bargain negotiations? If trial is the best alternative, you will need to determine the likely outcome of trial in order to know when to walk away from a settlement offer. In other words, you will need to determine the "expected value" of trial. How does one determine the expected value of trial?

> **Negotiation Nugget**
>
> Negotiators use many tools to determine the "expected value" of trial from decision-trees to data analytics. For more on decision trees, see Marjorie Aaron, RISK & RIGOR: A LAWYER'S GUIDE TO DECISION TREES FOR ASSESSING CASES AND ADVISING CLIENTS (2019). For more on data analytics, see Chapter 7.

3. In the transactional context, you will determine your BATNA (or your "perceived" BATNA) by looking at other options, sometimes referred to as "comparables"—e.g., other acceptable houses in the neighborhood in which you wish to live, other acceptable positions in the sorts of firms you wish to join, other potential business partners for the commercial venture you hope to start. Of course, as part of the decision-making process you will also need to determine and account for the cost of achieving your BATNA.

> **Negotiation Nugget**
>
> For an in-depth discussion of the expected value of a negotiator's BATNA, as well as WATNA, or worst alternative to a negotiated agreement; MLATNA, or most likely alternative to a negotiated agreement; AATNA, or any alternative to a negotiated agreement see a conversation among Hiro Aragaki, Sanda Kauffman, and John Lande on Indisputably, the ADR Professors blog
>
> Lande—Do you use BATNA wrong http://www.indisputably.org/?p=11632
>
> Kauffman—Of ATNAs and BATNAs http://www.indisputably.org/wp-content/uploads/Indisputably-199-Sandas-response_2.pdf
>
> Aragaki—Things We Think We Know About BATNA and WATNA http://www.indisputably.org/?p=12081
>
> Lande—Confusing Dispute Resolution Jargon http://www.indisputably.org/?p=12072

4.   The strength of a negotiator's BATNA stems from her interests. The better a BATNA meets a negotiator's interests, the better the BATNA. For example, in the real estate context, consider a buyer who has an interest in a shorter commute. The buyer is looking at a new home that costs $200,000 and that is 10 minutes from work. The buyer's BATNA is another home that costs $180,000 but is farther away from work. Is this BATNA strong, moderate, or weak based on its ability to meet the buyer's interest?

5.   Is it possible for a negotiator to improve her BATNA? If so, how does one go about doing so?

6.   Negotiators need to do their best to assess their counterpart's BATNA. As with assessing a counterpart's interests and likely preferred objective criteria, this requires thinking from the counterpart's perspective about alternatives. This exercise can help negotiators assess the counterpart's desire for an agreement and the parties' relative leverage. These assessments can lead to important information gathering strategies.

7.   Professor James K. Sebenius cautions negotiators against thinking that their BATNA "does *not* involve negotiation, that it should mainly be thought of as an *outside option independent of the other side*, and that it is primarily a *last resort* or only relevant if you feel weak." He argues instead that negotiators should think about their "best alternative with respect to a specific counterpart, a particular proposed agreement or class of agreements, and/or a definite time period or stage in the negotiation process." He distinguishes three different ways in which a negotiator might say "no" and the interplay of such moves with the negotiator's BATNA:

> **Note**
>
> Information gathering and information exchange are topics discussed later in Chapter 3.

First is a "tactical no," simply turning down a proffered deal in hopes of generating a better offer later in the process.

Second, is a "no to re-set." . . . [T]his "no" may occur at any stage of the process. It can entail moves "away from the table" to improve your own no-deal option and/or worsen that of the other side. You often employ the "no to re-set" with the intention of continuing to bargain or returning to active negotiation with your original counterpart, but in a setup that you have more actively modified to be more conducive to reaching your preferred deal.

Third, you may utter and mean a "final no," or the course of action you'd take if a sufficiently desirable agreement simply does not seem feasible with your counterpart.

If and when you utter a "tactical no," a "no to re-set," or a "final no," you should assess the implications by analyzing the same questions: how do you envision and evaluate the process playing out from the point of actually conveying your "no"? What does this mean for your minimum conditions going forward? Theirs? The prospects for a more favorable deal? And so on.

Jim Sebenius, *BATNAs in Negotiation: Common Errors and Three Kinds of "No"*, 33 Negot. J. 89, 97–98 (2017).

8.   A negotiator's BATNA can provide the negotiator with a source of power or situational advantage in negotiation. As Fisher, Ury, and Patton put it, "People think of negotiating power as being determined by resources like wealth, political connections, physical strength, friends, and military might. In fact, the relative negotiating power of two parties depends primarily upon how attractive to each is the option of not reaching agreement." Id. at 102.

For example, it is easily understood that a job applicant who already has another job or offer has more power in a job interview. But the same principle obtains in less obvious situations. Consider, for example, that you want to buy a new television. You go into your nearby big-box store and find just what you are looking for at a cost of $2,999, plus installation kit. You can give yourself additional power in the negotiation with the store by learning how much you would pay if you purchased the

> **Negotiation Nugget**
>
> Situational advantage in negotiation is more colloquially known as leverage, which is discussed below.

item elsewhere, such as through an online retailer or nearby store, and then exercise your power by asking the retailer if it will match the price you found elsewhere.

9.   Professor Russell Korobkin offers the important observation that it is one's perceived BATNA, as opposed to one's actual BATNA, that is the true source of power in negotiation. Russell Korobkin, *Bargaining Power as Threat of Impasse*, 87 Marq. L. Rev. 867, 869–70 (2004). Why might that be?

10.   We can think of power in negotiation as the ability to get what we want. A related concept is leverage—that is, the ability to use power or the situation to your advantage in a negotiation. Professor Shell offers the following easy-to-remember test to assess which party has more leverage in a negotiation:

Ask yourself, as of the moment when you make the assessment, which party has the most to lose from no deal. The party with the most to lose has the least leverage; the party with the least to lose has the most leverage; and both parties have roughly equal leverage when they both stand to lose equivalent amounts should the deal fall through.

G. RICHARD SHELL, BARGAINING FOR ADVANTAGE: NEGOTIATION STRATEGIES FOR REASONABLE PEOPLE 104 (2d ed. 2006). Note that the party with the least to lose is not always the party that appears to have more money, resources, and power.

D. THE NEGOTIATOR'S DILEMMA

One of the most fundamental features of negotiation is what is known as the Negotiator's Dilemma, which at its essence is how negotiators must engage in two separate but complementary negotiation tasks—claiming or distributing value, often described as "dividing the pie," and potentially creating new value from the opportunities that the negotiation presents, often described as "expanding the pie." Which task a negotiator emphasizes can vary by negotiation or even issue by issue within a negotiation. The questions of how to engage in each task, which task should receive more focus, and how these two tasks push and pull against each other consume most of the discussions concerning negotiation.

1. The Negotiator's Dilemma as a Theoretical Construct

JAMES K. SEBENIUS, NEGOTIATION ANALYSIS: A CHARACTERIZATION AND REVIEW
38 Management Science 18, 28–30 (Jan. 1992)

The lure of joint action lies in the prospect of each party's doing better than its alternatives to agreement. It is therefore crucial to understand the bases for joint gains and to envision possible agreements. In most negotiations, the potential value of joint action is *not* fully obvious at the outset.

Creating Value. "Creating value"—that is, reaching mutually beneficial agreements, improving them jointly, and preventing conflict escalation— requires an approach often associated with "win-win," "integrative," or "variable sum" encounters. To generate gainful options, it is normally helpful for information to be shared openly, communication enhanced, creativity spurred, joint problem-solving emphasized, and hostilities productively channeled. Many analysts offer insights into "creating value" by cooperative behavior. Regardless of whether one adopts a cooperative style or not, it is useful to have an analytic guide as to the underlying bases for joint gains. Three distinct classes of factors are at the core of all possible mutual benefits from cooperation; these factors are the raw material from which negotiators can "create value."

First, apart from pure shared interests, negotiators may want the same settlement on some issues, and their mere agreement may be able to produce it. Furthering their relationship, or acting in accord with an identical interest, such as a shared vision, ideology or norm of equity, may create value in an agreement. Interests, such as "good relationships," are analogous to the economist's "public goods" in that all sides can simultaneously "consume" them without diminution.

Second, where economies of scale, collective goods, alliances, or requirements for a minimum number of parties exist, agreement among similar bargainers can create value.

Third, though many people instinctively seek "common ground" and believe that "differences divide us," it is often precisely the *differences* among negotiators that constitute the raw material for creating value. Each class of difference has a characteristic type of agreement that makes possible its conversion into mutual benefit. For example, differences in relative valuation suggest joint gain from trades or from "unbundling" differently valued attributes. Differences in tax status, liquidity, or market access suggest arbitrage. Complementary technical capacities can be profitably combined. Probability and risk aversion differences suggest contingent agreements or bets. Differences in time preference suggest altering schedules of payments and other actions. . . . These observations point up value of a "differences orientation" with knowledge of the characteristic "technologies" for converting differences into mutual benefit.

* * *

Claiming Value. Crucial aspects of most negotiations, however, are primarily "distributive," "win-lose," or constant-sum; that is, at some points in the process, increased value claimed by one party implies less for others. For example, in choosing a strategy for the highly restrictive class of negotiations involving "first and final offers," one must balance the value to be claimed against the chance and cost of impasse. Although value can be created merely by reaching an accord in some cases, the parties' interests can conflict diametrically over the terms. And where value can be created by moves beyond the most obvious agreements that value must still be apportioned. Several broad classes of tactics used for "claiming value" in these kinds of bargains have been explored. Such tactics include: shaping perceptions of alternatives to agreement, making commitments, influencing aspirations, taking strong positions, manipulating patterns of concessions, holding valued issues "hostage," linking issues and interests for leverage, misleading other parties, as well as exploiting cultural and other expectations.

By means of these tactics, one party seeks advantage by influencing another's perceptions of the bargaining range.

Managing the Tension Between Creating and Claiming Value: The Negotiators' Dilemma. If the processes of creating and claiming value were separable, it would be possible to analyze and prescribe a separate approach to each task. Unfortunately, the fact that in general they are not undermines much otherwise useful advice (that, for example, presumes "win-win" situations to have no "win-lose" aspects, or "integrative" bargains to be unrelated to "distributive" ones) . . . .

> **Negotiation Nugget**
>
> The Pareto frontier is the set of options that achieve pareto efficiency or pareto optimality, where maximum value is created such that no one individual can be made better off without claiming value from another individual.

This has potent consequences for negotiation analysis. In general, the benefits of cooperation are not fully known at the outset of a negotiation. Moreover, the manner by which parties try to create value, or press out toward the potential Pareto frontier, normally influences the allocation of that value. Approaches that tend to be effective in claiming value tend to be highly dysfunctional for creating it. Yet, openness and information revelation aimed at value creating can be exploited by a "value claimer." Colloquially, the parties often do not know how large a pie they can make. The way in which they attempt to expand the pie often affects its final division, while each side's efforts to get a larger share of the pie often prevent its expansion in the first place—and may lead to no pie at all, or even to a fight.

Each party tends to reason over the course of an encounter as follows: If the other parties are open and forthcoming, I can take advantage of them and claim a great deal of value; thus I should adopt a value-claiming stance. By contrast, if the other parties are tough and adopt value-claiming stances, I must also adopt such a stance in order to protect myself. Either way, a strong tendency operating on all parties often leads to the result that *competitive moves to claim value individually drive out cooperative moves to create it jointly.* Outcomes of this dynamic include poor agreements, dead locks, and conflict spirals. This tendency, closely related in structure to the famous prisoner's dilemma, was dubbed the "Negotiator's Dilemma."

In analyzing the large number of tactics, approaches, and procedures offered to improve the effectiveness of negotiation, it is useful to focus on how a given suggestion manages the inherent tension between creating and claiming value. Many approaches naively ignore or deny the tension by simply advocating either a "win-win" or a "win-lose" philosophy. Yet, consider the successful characteristics of a tit-for-tat approach as analyzed by Robert Axelrod. To be *forthcoming* permits the exchange of information essential to get the joint process of creating value underway; to be provocable prevents exploitation of this openness by a value-claimer; while being *forgiving* looks beyond a forceful response to attempted exploitation to getting the cooperative process back on track, rather [than] seeing it escalate. In short, this approach offers one coherent response to managing the creating/claiming tension.

POINTS FOR DISCUSSION

1.   When speaking about the interaction of creating and claiming value, the term "value" is often misunderstood simply as the financial value in the transaction. Professors Deepak Malhotra and Max H. Bazerman describe value as "whatever people find useful or desirable" and contend that it can be measured by numerous metrics, including happiness and utility, in addition to dollars. DEEPAK MALHOTRA & MAX BAZERMAN, NEGOTIATION GENIUS: HOW TO OVERCOME OBSTACLES AND ACHIEVE BRILLIANT RESULTS AT THE BARGAINING TABLE AND BEYOND 16 (2007). What other metrics might one use to measure value? How does one measure happiness or utility?

2.   Methods of creating value in negotiation often focus on leveraging differences between the negotiating parties such as their valuations of good or services, expectations about the future, time preferences, priorities, and comfort levels with risk. How does focusing on these issues help create value? Professors Malhotra and Bazerman also suggest thinking about other methods, such as using contingency contracts, adding issues to the negotiation, and logrolling. Logrolling is simply the act of trading across issues, which is easier the more issues there are in a negotiation. DEEPAK MALHOTRA & MAX BAZERMAN, NEGOTIATION GENIUS: HOW TO OVERCOME OBSTACLES AND ACHIEVE BRILLIANT RESULTS AT THE BARGAINING TABLE AND BEYOND 61 (2007). Professors Robert R. Mnookin and Scott C. Peppet and Mr. Andrew S. Tulumello identify two other areas for creating value—taking advantage of non-competitive similarities, interests that truly do not compete, and economies of scale and scope. ROBERT H. MNOOKIN, SCOTT C. PEPPET & ANDREW S. TULUMELLO, BEYOND WINNING: NEGOTIATING TO CREATE VALUE IN DEALS AND DISPUTES 16 (2000). What else might help create value in a negotiation? What are economies of scope and scale?

3.   Once the value is created, what are the rules associated with claiming value? Should it be divided equally, equitably, or some other way? Without clear principles to determine the distribution, the negotiation may become a highly competitive endeavor. How should negotiators best proceed in this portion of the negotiation? See Morton Deutsch, *Equity, Equality, and Need: What Determines Which Value Will Be Used as the Basis of Distributive Justice?*, 31 J. Soc. Issues 137 (Summer 1975); David M. Messick, *Equality, Fairness, & Social Conflict*, 8 Soc. Just. Res. 153 (1995).

4.   In a passage in the book THE MANAGER AS NEGOTIATOR, where David Lax and James Sebenius first described the Negotiator's Dilemma, they say:

> Creating value requires openness, communication, learning, ingenuity, joint problem solving, and preventing conflict escalation. Claiming value involves advantageously shaping opponents' perceptions of the bargaining range, often by manipulating alternatives and aspirations, making commitments, holding prime values hostage, misleading, and exploiting cultural expectations.

Id. at 154. How is it that creating and claiming value can be bound together when the two are described in such Jekyll and Hyde terms? Does the authors' terminology suggest a preference for value creation over value claiming? If there is such a stark difference in creating and claiming value, how does one smoothly shift from one to the other?

2.   The Negotiator's Dilemma in Practice

In this subsection we take a closer look at value claiming and value creation, and at their implications for how negotiators approach the task of negotiating. Negotiators need to master both tasks, which requires them to understand how each task works and how to blend them to work together.

Generally speaking, when claiming value, negotiators are engaged in distributing what is assumed to be a limited resource—such as money, golf balls, or lima beans—and the parties' task is to decide whether and how to divide it. In such a situation, the parties' positions conflict; what one gains, the other must lose. The negotiators are, in a word, adversaries. When emphasizing value claiming, a negotiator naturally fosters strategies designed to maximize the client's position with respect to the resource in question. And typical tactics include those designed to uncover as

Digging Deeper

This distributive task is what most people think of when they think of negotiation. Why is this so?

much as possible about the other side's situation and simultaneously mislead the other side as to the negotiator's own situation.

Emphasizing value creation is quite different. The negotiators acknowledge that they share, and must solve, a problem. This approach seeks to create joint gains by meeting the interests or underlying needs of all parties to the dispute or transaction, and, accordingly, tends to produce strategies designed to promote the disclosure and relevance of these underlying needs. The recommended techniques include those intended to increase the number of issues for bargaining or to "expand the pie" before dividing it. Negotiation experts disagree as to whether it is possible to create value in every—or even the vast majority of—negotiations, but they do agree that a common feature of negotiation is the untapped potential for value creation.

Much of the negotiation literature makes it sound like the approach to negotiation is an either-or proposition. Either you are a negotiator who focuses on things like claiming value or you are a negotiator who focuses on things like creating value. By now you should understand that we disagree with such views: we believe that negotiators need to be good at the tasks associated with both claiming and creating value. While we may generally emphasize value creation, because we would like to see negotiators achieve more optimal solutions and because it tends to be a new concept to negotiation students, we recognize that all negotiators need to engage in value claiming.

Below, we introduce three generalized approaches to negotiation—one based on claiming value, another based on creating value, and a third, a hybrid mixing the two approaches, where negotiators attempt to be balanced by trying not to appear to favor one side of the negotiator's dilemma over the other. Legal negotiators should be acquainted with all three approaches because they most certainly will encounter and use all of them in practice.

a.   Value Claiming

In the following excerpt, Professor Russel Korobkin focuses on the distributive issues associated with negotiation, critical matters for value-claiming in negotiation.

RUSSELL KOROBKIN, A POSITIVE THEORY OF LEGAL NEGOTIATION
88 Geo. L. J. 1789, 1792–94 (2000)

In any negotiation, the maximum amount that a buyer will pay for a good, service, or other legal entitlement is called his "reservation point" or, if the deal being negotiated is a monetary transaction, his "reservation price" (RP). The minimum amount that a seller would accept for that item is her RP. If the buyer's RP is higher than the seller's, the distance between the two points is called the "bargaining zone." Reaching agreement for any amount that lies within the bargaining zone is superior to not reaching an agreement for both parties, at least if they are concerned only with the transaction in question.

For example, suppose Esau, looking to get into business for himself, is willing to pay up to $200,000 for Jacob's catering business, while Jacob, interested in retiring, is willing to sell the business for any amount over $150,000. This difference between Esau's and Jacob's RPs creates a $50,000 bargaining zone. At any price between $150,000 and $200,000, both parties are better off agreeing to the sale of the business than they are reaching no agreement and going their separate ways.

The same structure used to describe a transactional negotiation can be used to describe a dispute resolution negotiation. Suppose that Goliath has filed suit against David for battery. David is willing to pay up to $90,000 to settle the case out of court—essentially, to buy Goliath's legal right to bring suit—while Goliath will "sell" his right for any amount over $60,000. These RPs create a $30,000 bargaining zone between $60,000 and $90,000. Any settlement in this range would leave both parties better off than they would be without a settlement.

In contrast, if the seller's RP is higher than the buyer's RP, there is no bargaining zone. In this circumstance, there is no sale price that would make both parties better off than they would be by not reaching a negotiated agreement. Put another way, the parties would be better off not reaching a negotiated agreement. If Jacob will not part with his business for less than $150,000 and Esau will not pay more than $100,000 for it, there is no bargaining zone. If David will pay up to $50,000 to settle Goliath's claim, but Goliath will not accept any amount less than $60,000, again there is no bargaining zone. An agreement in either case would leave at least one party, and possibly both parties, worse off than if they were to decide not to make a deal.

> **Note**
>
> Notice that Professor Korobkin is discussing negotiators determining their reservation points, a critical part of negotiation preparation discussed in Chapter 3.

Knowledge of the parameters of the bargaining zone, which is created by the two parties' reservation points, is the most critical information for the negotiator to possess. Those parameters tell the negotiator both whether any agreement is possible and, if so, identify the range of possible deal points. At the same time, the negotiator has an interest in adjusting the parameters of the bargaining zone to his advantage. A buyer not only wants to know his and the seller's RP, he wishes to make both lower, or at least make both appear lower to the seller. This shifts the zone of possible deal points lower, increasing the chances that the seller will ultimately agree to a relatively low price. Experimental evidence in fact confirms that negotiators with more favorable RPs (that is, lower for buyers, higher for sellers) reach more profitable agreements than negotiators with less favorable RPs.

> **Negotiation Nugget**
>
> Platforms such as *SmartSettle One* provide negotiators a technological solution to quickly and easily determine if there is a positive bargaining zone without revealing their reservation points to each other.

Esau wants to know his and Jacob's RPs, but he also would like to shift both numbers, and therefore the bargaining range, lower. Assuming Esau knows his RP is $200,000 and learns Jacob's is $150,000, Esau knows that an agreement is possible for some amount greater than the latter figure and less than the former. If he could reduce Jacob's RP to $120,000 and his own to $170,000, however, the bargaining zone would remain the same size, but its changed parameters would suggest that Esau would be likely to buy the business for a lower price. Esau could achieve the same advantage if Jacob believes the parties' RPs are $120,000 and $170,000 respectively, even if the RPs objectively are $150,000 and $200,000.

The existence of a bargaining zone is necessary for a negotiated agreement, and the parameters of the bargaining zone—defined by both parties' RPs—define the set of possible "deal points."

POINTS FOR DISCUSSION

1.   The value-claiming focus is based on certain assumptions:

- That the principal goal of each party is to maximize its own economic gain;

- That the outcome of the negotiation will likely be determined by two separate, individualistic cost-benefit analyses, rather than through any joint exploration of what is most suitable for both parties;

- That the process will be closed and deceptive, with each party trying to mislead or at least to conceal information about its own position while seeking to learn as much as it can about the other's position; and

- That "deal points" fall along a continuum, and movement favorable to one party is inevitably unfavorable to the other.

Do you believe these assumptions to be accurate? Are there any other assumptions embedded in this approach? What should a negotiator with this focus do if these assumptions turn out to be unfounded?

2.   Commentators have used different terms when categorizing negotiators whose primary focus in negotiation is consistent with the tasks associated with the value-claiming aspects of negotiation. For example, some have labeled these activities the "adversarial" approach to negotiation. It has also been described as the "positional" approach to negotiation. *See* ROGER FISHER, WILLIAM URY & BRUCE PATTON, GETTING TO YES: NEGOTIATING AGREEMENT WITHOUT GIVING IN (3d ed. 2011). To see it described as "distributive," see DAVID LAX & JAMES SEBENIUS, THE MANAGER AS NEGOTIATOR: BARGAINING FOR COOPERATION AND COMPETITIVE GAIN (1986); HOWARD RAIFFA, THE ART AND SCIENCE OF NEGOTIATION (1982). Regardless of the label employed, when focusing on claiming value, negotiators often engage in zero-sum thinking in which the gains one side receives are at the expense of the other.

Negotiation Nugget

Zero-sum thinking is a cognitive bias that can misperceive situations as a zero-sum game and limit available options because of the false belief that one side's gain is the other side's loss.

3.   If the negotiator's reservation points overlap, meaning that the lowest price the seller will accept is lower than the highest price the buyer will pay, there is a positive bargaining range or zone of possible agreement (ZOPA), and the parties should be able to reach an agreement. Using distributive bargaining strategies such as anchoring, aspirational thinking, and objective criteria, negotiators can effectively claim more value within the ZOPA. However, if the negotiators' reservation points do not overlap and there is no ZOPA, the negotiators should pursue their respective BATNAs. Besides ethical issues, why might it be disadvantageous for a negotiator to misrepresent his reservation point?

4.   Critiques of excessive focus on value claiming in negotiation typically emphasize the negative effects of refusing to share information—e.g., inefficient outcomes or no deal when there should be one. *See generally* ROGER FISHER, WILLIAM URY & BRUCE PATTON, GETTING TO YES: NEGOTIATING AGREEMENT WITHOUT GIVING IN (3d ed. 2005); G. RICHARD SHELL, BARGAINING FOR ADVANTAGE: NEGOTIATION STRATEGIES FOR REASONABLE PEOPLE (2d ed. 2006); Robert H. Mnookin, *Strategic Barriers to Dispute Resolution: A Comparison of Bilateral and Multilateral Negotiations*, 8 Harv. Neg. L. Rev. 1, 4–7 & 11–14 (2003). Professor Catherine Tinsley and her colleagues found that competition and incentives to refrain from disclosing information result in less than optimal negotiation results for all parties. Catherine Tinsley, Kathleen M. O'Connor & Brandon A. Sullivan, *Tough Guys Finish Last: The Perils of a Distributive Reputation*, 88 Org. Beh. & Human Decision Processes 621, 621 (2002). Professor Andrea Kupfer Schneider studied the effectiveness of legal negotiators and found that an overly reliant focus on claiming value was viewed as being one of the less effective methods of negotiation. Andrea Kupfer Schneider, *Shattering Negotiation Myths: Empirical Evidence on the Effectiveness of Negotiation Style*, 7 Harv. Neg. L. Rev. 143, 196 (2002). How would someone who is a proponent of a strong focus on value claiming in negotiation respond to these claims?

b.   Value Creating

In this excerpt, Professor Carrie Menkel-Meadow describes how the distributive issues in negotiation only respond to one kind of need, financial interests. She argues that negotiators should expand their horizons to focus on the underlying actual needs, which we would describe as interests, a focus that may result in the distributive issues in negotiation playing out in different ways.

CARRIE J. MENKEL-MEADOW, TOWARD ANOTHER VIEW OF LEGAL NEGOTIATION: THE STRUCTURE OF PROBLEM SOLVING
31 UCLA L. Rev. 754, 794–801 and 840 (1984)

Problem solving is an orientation to negotiation which focuses on finding solutions to the parties' sets of underlying needs and objectives. The problem-solving conception subordinates strategies and tactics to the process of identifying possible solutions and therefore allows a broader range of outcomes to negotiation problems.

* * *

Parties to a negotiation typically have underlying needs or objectives— what they hope to achieve, accomplish, and/or be compensated for as a result of the dispute or transaction. Although litigants typically ask for relief in the form of damages, this relief is actually a proxy for more basic needs or objectives. By attempting to uncover those underlying needs, the problem-solving model presents opportunities for discovering greater numbers of and better quality solutions. It offers the possibility of meeting a greater variety of needs both directly and by trading off different needs, rather than forcing a zero-sum battle over a single item.

The principle underlying such an approach is that unearthing a greater number of the actual needs of the parties will create more possible solutions because not all needs will be mutually exclusive. As a corollary, because not all individuals value the same things in the same way, the exploitation of differential or complementary needs will produce a wider variety of solutions which more closely meet the parties' needs.

* * *

It is also important to recognize that both parties have such needs. For example, in [a] personal injury case, the defendant may have the same need for vindication or retribution if he believes he was not responsible for the accident. In addition, the defendant may need to be compensated for his damaged car and injured body. He will also have needs with respect to how much, when and how he may be able to pay the monetary damages because of other uses for the money. A contract breaching defendant may have specific financial needs such as payroll, advertising, purchases of supplies, etc.; defendants are not always simply trying to avoid paying a certain sum of money to plaintiffs. In the commercial case, the defendant may have needs similar to those of the plaintiff: lost income due to the plaintiff's failure to pay on the contract, and, to the extent the plaintiff may seek to terminate the relationship with the defendant, a steady source of future business.

* * *

To the extent that negotiators focus exclusively on "winning" the greatest amount of money, they focus on only one form of need. The only flexibility in tailoring an agreement may lie in the choice of ways to structure monetary solutions, including one shot payments, installments, and structured settlements. By looking, however, at what the parties desire money for, there may be a variety of solutions that will satisfy the parties more fully and directly. For example, when an injured plaintiff needs physical rehabilitation, if the defendant can provide the plaintiff directly with rehabilitation services, the defendant may save money and the plaintiff may gain the needed rehabilitation at lower cost. In addition, if the defendant can provide the plaintiff with a job that provides physical rehabilitation, the plaintiff may not only receive income which could be used to purchase more rehabilitation, but be further rehabilitated in the form of the psychological self-worth which accompanies such employment. Admittedly, none of these solutions may fully satisfy the injured plaintiff, but some or all may be equally beneficial to the plaintiff, and the latter two may be preferable to the defendant because they are less costly.

Understanding that the other party's needs are not necessarily as assumed may present an opportunity for arriving at creative solutions. Traditionally, lawyers approaching negotiations from the adversarial model view the other side as an enemy to be defeated. By examining the underlying needs of the other side, the lawyer may instead see opportunities for solutions that would not have existed before based upon the recognition of different, but not conflicting, preferences.

An example from the psychological literature illustrates this point. Suppose that a husband and wife have two weeks in which to take their vacation. The husband prefers the mountains and the wife prefers the seaside. If vacation time is limited and thus a scarce resource, the couple may engage in adversarial negotiation about where they should go. The simple compromise situation, if they engage in distributive bargaining, would be to split the two weeks of vacation time spending one week in the mountains and one week at the ocean. This solution is not likely to be satisfying, however, because of the lost time and money in moving from place to place and in getting used to a new hotel room and locale. In addition to being happy only half of the time, each party to the negotiation has incurred transaction costs associated with this solution. Other "compromise" solutions might include alternating preferences on a year to year basis, taking separate vacations, or taking a longer vacation at a loss of pay. Assuming that husband and wife want to vacation together, all of these solutions may leave something to be desired by at least one of the parties.

By examining their underlying preferences, however, the parties might find additional solutions that could make both happy at less cost. Perhaps the husband prefers the mountains because he likes to hike and engage in stream fishing. Perhaps the wife enjoys swimming, sunbathing and seafood. By exploring these underlying preferences the couple might find vacation spots that permit all of these activities: a mountain resort on a large lake, or a seaside resort at the foot of mountains. By examining their underlying needs the parties can see solutions that satisfy many more of their preferences, and the "sum of the utilities" to the couple as a whole is greater than what they would have achieved by compromising.

In addition, by exploring whether they attach different values to their preferences they may be able to arrive at other solutions by trading items. The wife in our example might be willing to give up ocean fresh seafood if she can have fresh stream or lake trout, and so, with very little cost to her, the couple can choose another watersport where the hikes might be better for the husband. By examining the weight or value given to certain preferences the parties may realize that some desires are easily attainable because they are not of equal importance to the other side. Thus, one party can increase its utilities without reducing the other's. This differs from a zero-sum conception of negotiation because of the recognition that preferences may be totally different and are, therefore, neither scarce nor in competition with each other. In addition, if a preference is not used to "force" a concession from the other party (which as the example shows is not necessary), there are none of the forced reciprocal concessions of adversarial negotiation.

The exploitation of complementary interests occurs frequently in the legal context. For example, in a child custody case the lawyers may learn that both parties desire to have the children some of the time and neither of the parties wishes to have the children all of the time. It will be easy, therefore, to arrange for a joint custody agreement that satisfies the needs of both parties. Similarly, in a commercial matter, the defendant may want to make payment over time and the plaintiff, for tax purposes or to increase interest income, may desire deferred income.

* * *

. . . The creative problem-solving approach outlined here depends on two structural components: (1) identifying the parties' underlying needs and objectives, and (2) crafting solutions, first by attempting to meet those needs directly, and second, by attempting to meet more of those needs through expanding the resources available. By utilizing such a framework for negotiations, the parties should recognize the synergistic advantage of such an approach over the adversarial and manipulative strategies of zero-sum negotiations. Parties should be able to achieve solutions to disputes that would not have been possible in court-ordered resolutions.

Note

In this excerpt, Professor Menkel-Meadow also discusses coming up with potential options, a foundational task discussed in Chapter 3.

POINTS FOR DISCUSSION

1. The value-creation approach is based on certain assumptions:

-   That the principal goal for each party is to meet its underlying needs and interests rather than simply beating the other side;

-   That the outcome of the negotiation will likely be determined by a joint exploration of what is most appropriate for both parties;

-   That the process will be an open and creative one in which each party shares information with the other about its underlying needs and interests; and

-   That parties can produce joint gains by capitalizing on both shared and different interests.

Do you believe these assumptions to be accurate? Are there any other assumptions embedded in this approach? What should a negotiator with this orientation do if these assumptions turned out to be unfounded?

2. Commentators have used different terms when categorizing negotiators whose primary focus in negotiation is consistent with the tasks associated with the value-creating aspects of negotiation. For example, some have labeled these activities the "problem-solving" approach to negotiation. It has also been referred to as "principled," see Roger Fisher, William Ury & Bruce Patton, GETTING TO YES: NEGOTIATING AGREEMENT WITHOUT GIVING IN 84 (3d ed. 2011). To see it described as "integrative," see DAVID LAX & JAMES SEBENIUS, THE MANAGER AS NEGOTIATOR: BARGAINING FOR COOPERATION AND COMPETITIVE GAIN (1986); HOWARD RAIFFA, THE ART AND SCIENCE OF NEGOTIATION (1982). Regardless of the label employed, this approach posits that negotiation is a collaborative exercise in which the parties work together to satisfy their interests and create joint gains.

3. The most popular explanation of focusing on value creation in negotiation appears in ROGER FISHER, WILLIAM URY, & BRUCE PATTON, GETTING TO YES: NEGOTIATING AGREEMENT WITHOUT GIVING IN (3d ed. 2011). The authors instruct negotiators using this method to attempt to achieve a wise, efficient, and amicable outcome, not merely to maximize gains. In contrast to the value-claiming orientation—which focuses solely on the substance of the negotiation—the value-creation orientation focuses on the substance, the process, and the relationship between the negotiators.

4. Several criticisms have been leveled at too much focus on value creation in negotiation. Some scholars have questioned theorists' contention that integrative, or value-creating, opportunities are as abundant as suggested. See, e.g., Russell Korobkin, *A Positive Theory of Legal Negotiation*, 88 Geo. L.J. 1789 (2000); Gerald Wetlaufer, *The Limits of Integrative Bargaining*, 85 Geo. L.J. 369 (1996). Others claim that it fails to give sufficient weight to the distributive, or value-claiming, side of the

Negotiator's Dilemma. James J. White, *The Pros and Cons to Getting to Yes*, 34 J. Legal Ed. 115, 121 (1984), Russell Korobkin, *Against Integrative Bargaining*, 58 Case West. Res. L. Rev. 1323 (2008). How would a proponent of the value-creating approach to negotiation respond to these claims?

    5.   Professors Robert Mnookin and Scott Peppet, and Mr. Andrew S. Tulumello argue that there is tension between two components of a negotiator's approach—assertiveness and empathy—that seem to parallel the distinction between a value creating mindset and a value claiming mindset. They define empathy as "demonstrating an understanding of the other side's needs, interests, and perspective, without necessarily disagreeing." On the other hand, they define assertiveness as "[the] advocacy of one's own needs, interest, and perspective." ROBERT H. MNOOKIN, SCOTT R. PEPPET & ANDREW S. TULUMELLO, BEYOND WINNING: NEGOTIATING TO CREATE VALUE IN DEALS AND DISPUTES 47 (2000).

    Are these qualities really in tension? Can negotiators exhibit both empathy and assertiveness? It is worth observing that empathy has affective, cognitive, and behavioral dimensions. Professor Mnookin and his colleagues focus on the latter two dimensions. Experimental research suggests that negotiators able to exercise the cognitive component of empathy—that is, perspective-taking—obtain superior outcomes in negotiation. *See* Adam D. Galinsky, William W. Maddux, Debra Gilin & Judith B. White, *Why It Pays To Get Inside the Head of Your Opponent: The Differential Effects of Perspective Taking and Empathy in Negotiations*, 19 Psychol. Sci. 378, 378–84 (2008). Professor Alyson Carrel describes the tension between assertion and empathy as one that plays out between artificial intelligence and emotional intelligence, arguing that as technology is increasingly able to handle distributive components of negotiation, lawyers must increasingly focus on emotional intelligence and empathy in order to distinguish their value as counselors at law and problem-solvers. See *Legal Intelligence Through Artificial Intelligence Requires Emotional Intelligence: A New Competency Model for the 21st Century Legal Professional*, 35 Ga. St. U. L. Rev. 1153 (2019).

> **Digging Deeper**
>
> Do either of these foci—creating or claiming value—seem better able to address the behavioral, cognitive, and emotional dimensions of conflict?

c.   Mixing Approaches

    The following excerpt examines the use of multiple approaches while negotiating. Specifically, Professor Charles Craver argues that the most successful negotiators use a mix of value-creating and value-claiming approaches.

CHARLES B. CRAVER, THE IMPACT OF NEGOTIATOR STYLES ON BARGAINING INTERACTIONS

35 Am. J. Trial Advoc. 1, 10–13, 17 (2011)

Skilled negotiators are able to combine the most salient traits associated with the cooperative problem-solving and the competitive adversarial styles. They work to maximize their client's returns, but they endeavor to accomplish this objective in a courteous and seemingly cooperative manner. They appreciate the childhood admonition expressed by many parents that "you get more with honey than you do with vinegar." They also recognize the importance of expanding the overall pie divided between the bargaining parties. Unlike less-skilled bargainers, who think of negotiation interactions as "fixed pie" situations in which one side's gain is the other side's corresponding loss, skilled negotiators understand that in multi-issue interactions the participants usually value the various items quite differently. Even when the principal issue is money, the parties can agree to future payments or in-kind payments to generate more efficient final agreements. Adroit negotiators appreciate the inherent tension between "value creation" and "value claiming." Although they strive to claim more of the distributive items desired by both sides, they look for integrative terms valued more by one side than by the other in recognition of the fact that if these terms are resolved efficiently, both sides will achieve better results. They are quite open with respect to underlying client interests to enable the parties to look for areas of possible joint gain, but they frequently over- or under-state the degree to which their clients actually want the various items to enable them to obtain more of the joint surplus than they give to their opponents. If they think their adversaries really want several issues their side does not value highly, they may exaggerate their interest in those terms, making it appear that they are conceding more than they actually are. If their side really desires specific items they believe the opposing party does not consider important, they may understate their actual interest in those terms enabling them to obtain these items in exchange for less significant concessions.

> **Negotiation Nugget**
>
> Professor Craver is distinguishing between negotiation *style* (cooperative/competitive) and *approach* (value-creation/value-claiming).

Competitive problem-solvers recognize that if the parties maximize the way in which the integrative terms are resolved, it is easier for them to claim more of the distributive items. Although they may manipulate opponent perceptions with respect to the degree to which they value particular terms, they do not employ truly deceitful tactics. They realize a loss of credibility would seriously undermine their capacity to obtain beneficial accords. Even though they hope to obtain a greater share of the joint surplus, they are not win-lose competitive adversarial negotiators, nor are they the win-win cooperative problem-solvers they appear to be. As competitive problem-solvers, they employ a hybrid style which Ronald Shapiro and Mark Jankowski characterize as: "WIN-win: big win for your side, little win for theirs." They understand that the imposition of poor terms on their adversaries does not necessarily benefit their own clients. All other factors being equal, they wish to maximize opponent satisfaction, as long as this does not require significant concessions with respect to terms valued by their own side. At the conclusion of bargaining encounters, they do not compare the results they have achieved with those obtained by their adversaries. They instead ask themselves whether their clients like what they received.

Competitive problem-solvers appreciate the importance of negotiation process. Studies indicate that persons who believe the bargaining process has been fair and they have been treated respectfully are more satisfied with objectively less beneficial final terms than those with objectively more beneficial terms achieved through a process considered less fair and less respectful. This explains why proficient competitive problem-solvers always treat their adversaries with respect and act professionally. They are also careful at the conclusion of interactions to leave opponents with the feeling those persons obtained "fair" results.

Competitive problem-solvers do not work to maximize opponent returns for purely altruistic reasons. They appreciate the fact that such behavior most effectively enhances their ability to advance their own interests. They understand that they must offer their opponents sufficiently generous terms to induce those persons to accept the agreements they are proposing. If they fail to propose accords within opponent settlement ranges, no agreements will be achieved. They also want to be certain that adversaries will honor the terms agreed upon. If opponents experience post-agreement "buyer's remorse," they may refuse to effectuate those accords. The final consideration concerns the fact that attorneys often interact with the same opponents in the future. If those individuals feel that their current encounters have been pleasant and beneficial, they will look forward to future interactions with those persons.

* * *

Many proficient negotiators employ a hybrid competitive problem-solving style. They behave in a seemingly open and cooperative manner but are not entirely open, and they subtly employ manipulative techniques to obtain a greater share of the joint surplus. They behave in a courteous and professional manner in recognition of the fact that this behavior increases the likelihood of achieving their objectives. Although their opponents think they are behaving in a cooperative fashion, they admittedly employ disingenuous tactics to advance their interests. Opponents who do not appreciate the degree to which the competitive value-creating style may be employed successfully are likely to concede more than they should.

> **Digging Deeper**
>
> Professor Craver's article condones subtle deception in negotiation. Is there a problem with such deception in the negotiation context?

POINTS FOR DISCUSSION

1.   Professor Leonard Riskin has pointed out the downfalls of rigidly following one negotiation approach or another.

> [M]any negotiators demonstrate a rigid loyalty to a model or element, *as they understand it*. Of course, studying, teaching and training initially require a certain sustained engagement with a model in order for students to understand it. The [value-creating] model, in particular, engenders a good deal of passion, and many students embrace it with fervor. Sometimes they do so without enough discernment; thus, for instance, they may fail to recognize "the negotiator's dilemma," which arises because interest-based and position-based moves can interfere with one another. [The value-creating approach to] negotiation generally requires some openness about one's motivations and, accordingly, presents a risk of exploitation by a counterpart's adversarial moves. Likewise, conduct that is too adversarial cuts off opportunities for addressing interests. Managing the negotiator's dilemma requires that the negotiator be aware of this dilemma moment to moment and maintain an appropriate balance. This makes improvisation essential. And I believe that most skillful negotiators do improvise in this sense.

Leonard L. Riskin, *Beginning with Yes: A Review Essay of Michael Wheeler's* The Art of Negotiation: How to Improvise Agreement in a Chaotic World, 16 Cardozo J. Confl. Resol. 605, 614–18 (2015).

2.   Professors Gerald Williams and Charles Craver recommend employing the mixed approach to negotiation described above as follows:

> We believe that attorneys should work diligently to advance the interests of their own clients, but should not allow this objective to negate other equally important considerations, such as behaving ethically and professionally and seeking fair settlements that maximize the joint returns achieved by both sides. Once negotiators obtain what they think is appropriate for their own clients, they should look for ways to accommodate the non-conflicting interests of their opponents.

Digging Deeper

Professor Riskin suggests that negotiators be aware of the negotiator's dilemma moment to moment. How does one do this? One method to heighten one's awareness is through mindfulness meditation, which is discussed in Chapter 1.

GERALD WILLIAMS & CHARLES CRAVER, LEGAL NEGOTIATING 53 (2007). The quote above makes it sound like having an interest in maximizing joint returns, seeking fair settlements, or nurturing relationships is outside the realm of client interests. Could those be a client's interest as well?

3.   Keith G. Allred conducted an empirical study to determine best negotiation practices for managing the tension between creating and claiming value. Specifically, he identified several negotiation tactics that he said are *always* effective, that is, they transcend the claiming value—creating value spectrum because they do not diminish negotiation performance on other dimensions. A few of these practices include: developing and improving one's BATNA, using only the best arguments supporting the positions one advocates, working to see where one's interests are met, treating the other party with consideration and respect, engaging in a collaborative effort to fulfill both parties' underlying interests, and avoiding needless unpleasantness. See Keith G. Allred, *Distinguishing Best and Strategic Practices: A Framework for Managing the Dilemma between Claiming and Creating Value*, 16 Neg. J. 387 (2000).

4.   After reading the various excerpts in this section, what are your underlying assumptions about the negotiation process? Which approach do you favor? Why? Are there contexts where one approach is beneficial to the others?

E.   REPUTATION AND TRUST

It is often said that a good reputation is a lawyer's greatest asset. Likewise, a good reputation is a valuable asset for negotiators. A negotiator's reputation not only precedes him, it also impacts how others react to his statements and actions both inside and outside the negotiation process. For example, what will negotiators do if their counterpart has a reputation for throwing a fit in the middle of negotiations? Will the tantrum, if it occurs, have any impact?

> ### Negotiation Nugget
>
> "It takes many good deeds to build a good reputation, and only one bad one to lose it."
>
> — Benjamin Franklin

An interesting aspect of one's reputation as a negotiator is that it can change over time, albeit slowly, and it can be different among different people. But what is a reputation exactly? A common definition is "a coherent image of the nature of someone's character which then directs how that person will behave subject to situational restraints." Catherine H. Tinsley, Andrea Kupfer Schneider & Jack Cambria, *Reputations in Negotiation*, *in* 1 THE NEGOTIATOR'S DESK REFERENCE 251 (Andrea Kupfer Schneider & Christopher Honeyman eds., 2017). Another way to think of reputations is a "socially constructed label[ ] that extend[s] the consequences of a party's actions across time, situations or other actions." Catherine H. Tinsley, Kathleen M. O'Connor & Brandon A. Sullivan, *Tough Guys Finish Last: The Perils of a Distributive Reputation*, 88 Org. Beh. & Human Decision Processes. 621, 622 (2002). With these definitions in mind, what reputation should negotiators develop, and upon which criteria should they focus? And how can negotiators protect their reputations?

Note that in the following excerpt about negotiators' reputations, Professor Nancy Welsh discusses how one's negotiation style is correlated with trustworthiness and perceptions of a procedurally just process, all of which enhance one's reputation as a negotiator.

NANCY A. WELSH, THE REPUTATIONAL ADVANTAGES OF DEMONSTRATING TRUSTWORTHINESS: USING THE REPUTATION INDEX WITH LAW STUDENTS
28 Negot. J. 117, 136–139 (2011)

Exploring trustworthiness requires an initial look at the general concept of trust. Roger Mayer and his colleagues . . . defined trust as "the willingness of a party to be vulnerable to the actions of another party based on the expectation that the other will perform a particular action important to the trustor, irrespective of the ability to monitor or control that other party," and observed that "[b]eing vulnerable implies that there is something of importance to be lost."

Researchers have found in other professional, nonlegal contexts that the ability to create "an environment of trust" will play a significant role in achieving a negotiation's integrative potential. One hears echoes here of the research regarding the effects of perceptions of procedural justice in negotiation. Further, and in light of the correlations between perceptions of procedural justice and trustworthiness, it seems that a negotiator's perceived trustworthiness—or his/her ability to create an environment of trust—is likely to be positively correlated with his/her effectiveness as an integrative negotiator and not negatively correlated with his/her effectiveness as a distributive negotiator. This suggests that there is no disadvantage to behaving in a manner that is consistent with procedural justice and trustworthiness.

> **Note**
>
> Remember, the integrative potential of a negotiation is another way of referring to the opportunities the parties have to create value during the negotiation.

But the reality of legal negotiation—in which lawyers must play the simultaneous and conflicting roles of both adversaries and professional colleagues—suggests that lawyers will find it very difficult, if not ethically impossible, to offer *unconditional* trustworthiness to each other. Must lawyers, therefore, leave consideration of trustworthiness behind? Williams has urged for example that the legal negotiators who fit the aggressive pattern are hesitant to extend trust to anyone. They "recognize that one way to avoid being too soft is always to be hard negotiators; that way, they are never in danger of being too trusting. This saves them from the more difficult task of figuring out when and whom to trust[.]"

* * *

Legal negotiation is rife with conflicting relationships that have the potential to pull lawyers in opposing directions and suggest the value of thinking in terms of both calculus-based trust and even a degree of rational distrust. The relationship between lawyer and client can easily conflict with lawyers' shared commitments to their profession, to their colleagues in that profession, and to the justice system. Interestingly, the degree of this conflict may depend upon a lawyer's perception of how "deep" or "shallow" his/her relationship is with the profession, with other lawyers, and with the justice system—and whether "the profession" or "the justice system" is separate from, and has significance beyond, the individual lawyers (and judges) who are part of it. Perhaps paradoxically, the degree of the conflict also may depend upon the clarity with which society, the legal profession, disciplinary bodies, and courts have declared the lawyer's relationship with his/her client to be primary.

> **Note**
>
> Calculus-based trust is the kind of trust based on one's knowledge of the consequences of compliance or noncompliance with promised behaviors. It is discussed further in the notes following this excerpt.

* * *

Conclusion

Available research strongly suggests that lawyers with positive reputations as legal negotiators tend to be those perceived by their peers as skilled lawyers who maximize results for their clients *and* are sufficiently trustworthy. Such trustworthiness can be understood as an elastic yet meaningful concept that (1) incorporates both trust and distrust, (2) is bounded by lawyers' ethical obligations, (3) is distinct from any particular negotiation approach . . ., but (4) is more likely correlated with—that is, supporting and being supported by—a cooperative, procedurally just negotiation style.

POINTS FOR DISCUSSION

1.   Professor Welsh's article discusses trust and concludes that a negotiator should cultivate a reputation for trustworthiness. Trust is based on one's evaluation of another's ability, integrity, and benevolence. Roger C. Mayer, James H. Davis & F. David Schoorman, *An Integrative Model of Organizational Trust*, 20 Acad. Mgmt. Rev.

709, 717 (1995). According to Mayer and his colleagues, ability refers to the skills, knowledge, capabilities, and characteristics the individual has in a particular subject area or matter. Integrity is associated with adherence to a set of principles the would-be trustor finds acceptable, and benevolence is the degree to which the other individual has a positive inclination towards the would-be trustor. With these characteristics in mind, how does one cultivate a reputation for trustworthiness?

2.   If we are to understand trustworthiness, we need to have a good working definition of trust. Roy Lewicki and his colleagues have studied several dimensions of trust, which is defined as "an individual's belief in, and willingness to act on the basis of the words, actions, and decisions of another." Roy J. Lewicki & Carolyn Wiethoff, *Trust, Trust Development, and Trust Repair, in* THE HANDBOOK OF CONFLICT RESOLUTION: THEORY AND PRACTICE 106 (Morton Deutsch & Peter T. Coleman eds., 2000).

3.   Professors Roy Lewicki and Barbara Benedict Bunker report that there are three types of trust that build upon each other. The first is calculus-based trust, which is based on one's knowledge of the consequences of compliance or noncompliance with promised behaviors. For example, a settlement agreement to resolve a litigated matter typically requires the delivery of payment to resolve the claim as a prerequisite to the claim's dismissal. Knowing what could happen if a promise is not fulfilled, such as court filings to enforce the terms of the settlement agreement, typically results in the fulfilment of the contracted promises. The second is knowledge-based trust, which is based on

Digging Deeper

How does one regain trust once it has been broken? What steps does one have to take?

knowledge of another's characteristics and traits, such as reliability, through experience with that person. For example, a law firm partner may know through experience that her associate will ably handle a negotiation in her stead because the associate has proven his ability to do so time and again. The third kind of trust is identity-based trust. It is based on such complete identification, understanding, appreciation, and sharing of another's interests, desires, and intentions that one person can effectively act for the other. This is the type of trust that can develop in close friendships, spousal relationships, and long-standing attorney-client relationships, among other situations. Roy Lewicki & Barbara Benedict Bunker, *Trust in Relationships: A Model of Development and Decline, in* CONFLICT, COOPERATION & JUSTICE: ESSAYS INSPIRED BY THE WORK OF MORTON DEUTSCH 133 (Barbara Benedict Bunker & Jeffrey Z. Rubin eds., 1995).

4.   Lewicki and his colleagues have also written about another valuable dimension that appears to be the opposite of trust but is not necessarily so—distrust. Distrust is defined as "the confident expectation that another individual's motives, intentions, and behaviors are sinister and harmful to one's own interests." Roy J.

Lewicki, *Trust and Distrust*, *in* 1 THE NEGOTIATOR'S DESK REFERENCE 207 (Andrea Kupfer Schneider & Christopher Honeyman eds., 2017). In distrust situations, a belief that the other seeks to cause harm motivates protective measures. Calculus-based distrust is confident negative expectations of another's conduct where the costs of maintaining trust outweigh the benefits of maintaining trust. In such situations, the anticipated costs outweigh the benefits of the transaction, and looking for another to deal with becomes necessary. For example, suppose that your company is downsizing, you and a co-worker hold the same position, and your supervisor must decide who will keep their job. You meet first with the supervisor. Your co-worker's meeting is the next day. Will you tell your co-worker all of the questions asked by the supervisor? Why not? Is it because you don't like your co-worker? If it is impossible to avoid the situation, creating boundaries and systems for monitoring and enforcing performance become key. Identification-based distrust arises from perceptions of direct conflicts in values or goals or from negative emotions. In these situations, distrust can be almost visceral, as with warring families, tribes, or countries, and minimizing the interaction and any dependence on the other is best.

5.   While it is important to understand how trust works, psychologist David DeSteno reminds us that our trust calculations in real time are both conscious and subconscious. At the conscious level, we analyze another's behaviors and calculate or recalculate how much we trust someone. At the subconscious level, our calculations lead to a gut feeling or instinct about whether or how much we should trust another. When these two evaluations are in alignment, we act in accord with the conclusion. When they are not in alignment, DeSteno advises following the subconscious evaluation because "intuitive processes provide more accurate information than reflective ones." DAVID DESTENO, THE TRUTH ABOUT TRUST: HOW IT DETERMINES SUCCESS IN LIFE, LOVE, LEARNING, AND MORE 106–10 (2014). Do you think that intuitive judgments are always more accurate than more deliberate ones?

6.   DeSteno also notes that our reliance on reputations serves as a prime method for solving problems of trust. Rather than having to guess about another's trustworthiness, we rely on other people's experiences with that person to determine whether to trust that individual. *Id.* at 15.

7.   In one study of non-lawyers, Professor Catherine Tinsley and her colleagues found that reputations impacted negotiators' perceptions of a counterpart's intentions, negotiators' own behaviors, and the negotiation outcomes. In group negotiations where one negotiator had a reputation as an adept distributive negotiator (i.e., having an ability to extract concessions), the negotiators spent more time sharing general information and less time discussing specific information about priorities and preferences, engaged in more small talk, and made more procedural remarks than in groups where the negotiators had no information about their counterpart's reputation. Negotiators whose counterparts had a reputation as

distributive negotiators judged those counterparts' intentions as less favorable than did negotiators whose counterparts had no reputation. And, negotiation pairs where one party had a distributive reputation achieved lower joint gains than those pairs in which the parties had no reputational information. Catherine Tinsley, Kathleen M. O'Connor & Brandon A. Sullivan, *Tough Guys Finish Last: The Perils of a Distributive Reputation*, 88 Org. Beh. & Human Decision Processes 621, 621 (2002).

8.   In another study of non-lawyers, Professor Kathleen M. O'Connor and her colleagues found that prior negotiation experiences had an impact on subsequent negotiations. Negotiators were asked to complete two negotiations. Negotiators who reached an agreement in their first negotiation were more likely to reach agreement in a second negotiation than those whose first negotiation resulted in impasse. In other words, impasse in the initial negotiation made impasse in the second negotiation more likely. This was true when negotiators had the same counterparts in both negotiations and when they were paired with different counterparts in the second negotiation. Some negotiators who reached impasse in their first negotiation did reach agreement in the second negotiation. But the terms of these deals were not as good as the deals negotiated by those who reached agreement in the first negotiation. In fact, the more cooperative the negotiators were in their initial negotiation, the higher their outcomes were in the subsequent negotiation. Kathleen M. O'Connor, Josh A. Arnold & Ethan R. Burris, *Negotiators' Bargaining Histories and Their Effects on Future Negotiation Performance*, 90 J. App. Psych. 350 (2005).

> **Digging Deeper**
>
> Many social science studies look at the behavior of college-aged adults, that is 18–22 years of age. Maybe you participated in such research while in college. Do you think that age group is representative of all adults? What about people who work in the professions?

9.   Some research suggests that in certain contexts, a reputation as a very aggressive legal negotiator can produce superior outcomes for clients. In other contexts, aggressiveness seems to make no difference or to be counterproductive. The devil is in the details, though. Aggressiveness might be defined in terms of a particular bargaining style or, instead, be associated with making aggressive use of legal procedures and developing other options. See D. James Greiner, Cassandra Wolos Pattanayak & Jonathan Hennessy, *The Limits of Unbundled Legal Assistance: A Randomized Study in a Massachusetts District Court and Prospects for the Future*, 126 Harv. L. Rev. 901, 919 (2013).

10.   Managing one's reputation is a complex and necessary task. How does one keep reputation in mind in the midst of a negotiation? Do people have accurate impressions of their negotiation reputations? If not, how should they go about improving their assessments?

11.   Another approach to reputation while negotiating is to "Separate the Person from the Problem." Professor Fisher and Messrs. Ury and Patton suggest that a principled negotiator refrains from attacking the other negotiator, but instead shifts all their attention to the issues being negotiated.

Digging Deeper

Some lawyers like to cultivate tough competitive reputations as a method of intimidation or to attract clients who want a "bulldog" to represent them. As you continue through this book, ask yourself whether this is a wise decision.

Separate the emotional and interpersonal dynamics from the substantive issues on the table. ROGER FISHER, WILLIAM URY & BRUCE PATTON, GETTING TO YES: NEGOTIATING AGREEMENT WITHOUT GIVING IN 86 (3d ed. 2011). How might this enhance your reputation as a negotiator?

12.   Does the notion of separating the people from the problem conflict with a lawyer's duty to zealous advocacy? The comments to Rule 1.3 of the Model Rules of Professional Conduct require lawyers to represent their client with zeal but go on to explain that this zealous representation "does not require the use of offensive tactics or preclude the treating of all persons involved in the legal process with courtesy and respect."

CHAPTER 3

THE NEGOTIATION PROCESS

Every negotiation is unique, with its own environment and variables: the issues, the parties, the lawyers, the interests, the parties' respective leverage, and on and on. Professor Michael Wheeler implores us to embrace the inherent chaos in negotiation and to recognize that "managing uncertainty should be the cornerstone of your negotiation strategy." THE ART OF NEGOTIATION: HOW TO IMPROVISE AGREEMENT IN A CHAOTIC WORLD 13 (2013). He suggests that negotiators continuously "learn, adapt, and influence." *Id.* at 1–4. To do this, negotiators need a sound understanding of negotiation theory and the negotiation process so they can make conscious choices in the moment.

Negotiation Nugget

In his book *The Art of Negotiation: How to Improvise Agreement in a Chaotic World*, Harvard Business School Professor Michael Wheeler says that negotiation should be considered a form of improvisation and compares it favorably to other forms of improvisation—jazz and comedy.

The first thing to understand about the negotiation process is that even though it can be fluid and unpredictable, most negotiations follow a somewhat predictable pattern. In the following excerpt, Professor Shell argues that negotiations typically include four steps or stages.

G. RICHARD SHELL, BARGAINING FOR ADVANTAGE: NEGOTIATION STRATEGIES FOR REASONABLE PEOPLE
119 (2d ed. 2006)

Negotiation is a dance that moves through four stages or steps. . . . Let's look at a simple example from real life to see how the four-step sequence works in practice.

Imagine you are approaching a traffic intersection in your car. You notice that another car is nearing the intersection at the same time. What do you do?

Most experienced drivers start by slowing down to assess the situation. Next, they glance toward the other driver to make eye contact, hoping to establish communication with the other person. With eye contact established, one driver waves his or her hand toward the intersection in the universally recognized "after you" signal. Perhaps both drivers wave. After a little hesitation, one driver moves ahead and the other follows.

Note the four-step process: preparation (slowing down), information exchange (making eye contact), proposing and concession making (waving your hand), and commitment (driving through). This may seem like a unique case, but anthropologists and other social scientists have observed a similar four-stage process at work in situations as diverse as rural African land disputes, British labor negotiations, and American business mergers. The four stages form an unstated and often unseen pattern just below the surface of negotiations.

POINTS FOR DISCUSSION

1.   Professor Shell's depiction of the negotiation process as four steps can be viewed as a bare minimum, and it is one that we suggest in this book, although we alter it just slightly using "offers and concessions" for "concession making." Others parse the process more finely. For example, Professor Thomas Guernsey argues that negotiations generally include ten stages: (a) preparation and planning; (b) ice breaking; (c) agenda control; (d) information bargaining; (e) proposals, offers, demands; (f) persuasion/justification; (g) concessions/reformulation; (h) crisis (i.e., resolution or deadlock); (i) closing; and (j) memorialization. THOMAS F. GUERNSEY, A PRACTICAL GUIDE TO NEGOTIATION 12 (1996).

2.   Even though negotiations generally tend to flow from one stage to the next, it is useful to keep in mind that many negotiations are non-linear. It is common, for example, for negotiators to rush past the information exchange stage to start sharing offers and concessions. Or new information may come to light when finalizing a deal, resulting in a new round of offers and concessions. Or an individual may not realize she is in a negotiation until she is well into it, making preparation a wished-for impracticality. Additionally, some specific negotiation tasks bridge the four stages, as negotiators prepare strategies for exchanging information and making offers and concessions.

A.   PREPARATION

The biggest mistake that most negotiators make is failing to prepare adequately, or even at all. They believe their knowledge of the situation will suffice and that their experience or instincts are all they need to rely upon for success. If there is a logic here, it is overly simplistic—what worked before will work again. While there certainly can be similarities across negotiations, such logic is flawed: each negotiation has its own set of variables that make it unique. The importance of preparation cannot be understated; it is one of the easiest ways to increase your effectiveness as a negotiator. Planning for the unique challenges of each negotiation is what keeps the best negotiators at the top of their game.

Those who do minimal preparation tend to start from positions and work through logical arguments supporting those positions in the hope these arguments will win over their counterpart. They may spend some time considering the positions they expect their counterparts to advocate in the negotiation. Other negotiators reject this positional approach as being too limiting because it ignores the value creation side of the Negotiator's Dilemma. It is also important to plan an offer and concession strategy. Winging it is a clear invitation for ineffective behavior and mistakes that decrease the chances of reaching an agreement. For example, unprepared negotiators may be prone to cognitive biases such as confirmation bias, selective attention, and misattribution, as well as engage in unethical behavior such as lying about or failing to disclose material facts.

Any preparation efforts need to focus first on the negotiation fundamentals discussed in Chapter Two—considering interests to help create value as well as identifying objective criteria and a BATNA to guide the claiming of value. By identifying your interests before the negotiation, you can better assess the strength of your BATNA, determine the value of potential settlement options, and ensure you do not walk away from a good deal or accept a bad deal. Thorough preparation also includes considering your counterpart's interests and likely BATNA, along with the objective criteria your counterpart is likely to employ. Anticipating these elements will assist with other preparation tasks discussed below.

1.   Reservation Points and Goals

A negotiator's reservation point is closely related to her BATNA because it delineates the point where her BATNA becomes more attractive than a potential deal. A goal can be thought of the highest legitimate expectation a negotiator can achieve. In the following excerpt, we revisit

Professor Korobkin's article discussing a more value claiming approach of negotiation. This excerpt focuses on reservation points and describes the interaction of one's reservation point and BATNA.

RUSSELL KOROBKIN, *A POSITIVE THEORY OF LEGAL NEGOTIATION*
88 Georgetown L. Rev. 1789, 1794–97 (2000)

A negotiator cannot determine his [reservation point (RP)] without first understanding his substitutes for and the opportunity costs of reaching a negotiated agreement.

* * *

If the negotiator's BATNA and the subject of the negotiation are perfectly interchangeable, determining the reservation price is quite simple: the reservation price is merely the value of the BATNA. For example, if Esau's BATNA is buying another catering business for $190,000 that is identical to Jacob's in terms of quality, earnings potential, and all other factors that are important to Esau, then his RP is $190,000. If Jacob will sell for some amount less than that, Esau will be better off buying Jacob's company than he would be pursuing his best alternative. If Jacob demands more than $190,000, Esau is better off buying the alternative company and not reaching an agreement with Jacob.

> **Note**
>
> This article is excerpted earlier in Chapter 2, and this passage presumes familiarity with the prior excerpt.

In most circumstances, however, the subject of a negotiation and the negotiator's BATNA are not perfect substitutes. If Jacob's business is of higher quality, has a higher earnings potential, or is located closer to Esau's home, he would probably be willing to pay a premium for it over what he would pay for the alternative choice. For example, if the alternative business is selling for $190,000, Esau might determine he would be willing to pay up to a $10,000 premium over the alternative for Jacob's business and thus set his RP at $200,000. On the other hand, if Esau's BATNA is more desirable to him than Jacob's business, Esau will discount the value of his BATNA by the amount necessary to make the two alternatives equally desirable values for the money; perhaps he will set his RP at $180,000 in recognition that his BATNA is $10,000 more desirable than Jacob's business, and Jacob's business would be equally desirable only at a $10,000 discount.

* * *

The relationship between a party's BATNA and his RP can be generalized in the following way. A party's RP has two components: (1) the market value of his BATNA; and (2) the difference *to him* between the value of his BATNA and the value of the subject of the negotiation. A seller sets his RP by calculating (1) and either *subtracting* (2) if the subject of the negotiation is more valuable than his BATNA (and therefore he is willing to accept less to reach an agreement) or *adding* (2) if the BATNA is more valuable than the subject of the negotiation (and therefore, he would demand more to reach an agreement and give up his BATNA). A buyer sets his RP by calculating (1) and either *adding* (2) if the subject of the negotiation is more valuable than his BATNA (and therefore he would pay a premium to reach an agreement) or *subtracting* (2) if his BATNA is more valuable than the subject of the negotiation (and therefore he would demand a discount to give up the BATNA).

> **Negotiation Nugget**
>
> A negotiator's subjective valuation comes into play when determining a reservation price. When discussing this with a client, attorneys should feel free to discuss this subjective valuation openly as it may help uncover unstated interests.

Internal preparation serves two related purposes. By considering the value of obvious alternatives to reaching a negotiated agreement, the negotiator can accurately estimate his RP. This is of critical importance because without a precise and accurate estimation of his RP the negotiator cannot be sure to avoid the most basic negotiating mistake—agreeing to a deal when he would have been better off walking away from the table with no agreement.

POINTS FOR DISCUSSION

1.   What is the best way to describe the difference between one's BATNA and one's reservation point? Does a reservation point have to be purely monetary?

2.   In the earlier excerpt of Professor Korobkin's article in Chapter 2, he points out that the parties' respective reservation points frame whether there is a bargaining zone, and he states that "knowledge of the parameters of the bargaining zone . . . is the most critical information for the negotiator to possess." Do you agree

with this statement? Why or why not? This statement also implies that a negotiator should try to estimate a counterpart's reservation point. What is the best method of doing that?

3. Note that Korobkin places a lot of weight on the valuation of a negotiator's BATNA while recognizing that BATNAs are not always perfect substitutes for the subject matter of the negotiation. How does one go about making valuations in these kinds of situations? Are they strictly subjective?

> **Note**
>
> The use of data analytics, and the inherent biases of data analytics, as a means of informing a negotiator's BATNA is discussed in Chapter 7.

Lawyers who use an *expected-value* approach rely on basic economic principles to help them determine their reservation point and BATNA. Consider how this might work in litigation. Suppose that a plaintiff has filed a breach of contract suit against a defendant for $100,000. Suppose further that the lawyers representing both litigants believe, based on the facts of the case and the legal research they have conducted, that the plaintiff has a 50% of winning. Finally, suppose that both litigants will have to spend $10,000 more to litigate the case to a verdict than they will to settle.

> **Negotiation Nugget**
>
> Two excellent discussions of the expected value approach using decision tree analysis are Marjorie Corman Aaron's book *Client Science: Advice for Lawyers on Counseling Clients through Bad News and Other Legal Realities* (2012) and John Lande, Michaela Keet, and Heather D. Heavin's *Litigation Interest and Risk Assessment: Help Your Clients Make Good Litigation Decisions* (2020).

To calculate the expected value of trial for the plaintiff, her lawyer multiplies the probability of prevailing (50%) by the anticipated judgment ($100,000) and subtracts the costs of trial ($10,000). The expected value of trial for the plaintiff is thus $40,000 [(50% × $100,000) + (50% × $0) – $10,000].

To calculate the expected value of trial for the defendant, her lawyer multiplies the probability of the plaintiff prevailing (50%) by the anticipated judgment (–$100,000) and subtracts the costs of trial ($10,000). The expected value of trial for the defendant under these circumstances is thus –$60,000 [(50% × –$100,000) + (50% × $0) – $10,000].

Based on these calculations, the plaintiff should be willing to settle for a minimum of $40,000, and the defendant should be willing to pay a maximum of $60,000 to settle. Thus, the lawyers should attempt to negotiate a settlement within this $20,000 bargaining range. The difficulty comes, of course, when the lawyers have vast disagreements on the probability of prevailing.

To calculate the expected value of trial, a lawyer must predict how a judge or jury will apply governing principles of law to the facts of the case. If a settlement offer or demand is better for the client than the expected value of trial, she will advise her client to settle; if it is not, she will recommend trial. Thus, a lawyer employing the expected-value approach to settlement bargains "in the shadow of the law." Robert H. Mnookin & Lewis Kornhauser, *Bargaining in the Shadow of the Law: The Case of Divorce*, 88 Yale L.J. 950 (1979).

4. Even though determining the expected value of a BATNA is an important part of preparation, there is no guarantee that it will determine the settlement amount or even that settlement will occur. What accounts for this? Professor Russell Korobkin and Dean Chris Guthrie challenge the conventional wisdom that settlements break down because of party miscalculation or disagreement over distribution; they suggest that psychological dynamics also play an important role. Russell Korobkin & Chris Guthrie, *Psychological Barriers to Litigation Settlement: An Experimental Approach*, 93 Mich. L. Rev. 107, 108–09 (1994). The following notes identify some of those psychological processes, often described as heuristics.

> **Negotiation Nugget**
>
> Think of this relationship between gains and losses in terms of a gambler at a casino. Once a gambler gets ahead, most of them seek to protect their winnings. But once they get behind, many start to make double-or-nothing bets, bets considered to be much risker because of the potential amount of losses.

   a. *Framing Effects.* When faced with risk or uncertainty—like when deciding whether to settle a case or go forward to trial—people tend to make risk-averse decisions when choosing between options that appear to be gains and risk-seeking decisions when choosing between options that appear to be losses. See, e.g., Jeffrey J. Rachlinski, *Gains, Losses, and the Psychology of Litigation*, 70 S. Cal. L. Rev. 113, 128–29 (1996) (discussing prospect theory).

   b. *Self-Serving Biases.* When evaluating their respective cases, litigants and lawyers may overestimate their chances of prevailing at trial due to "self-serving" or "egocentric" biases. Chris Guthrie, Jeffrey J. Rachlinski & Andrew J. Wistrich, *Inside the Judicial Mind*, 86 Cornell L. Rev. 777, 811–13 (2001).

Negotiation Nugget

One famous example of a self-serving/egocentric bias was a study where law students were assigned to play the role of the plaintiff and defendant in an automobile-motorcycle collision case where the plaintiff was seeking $100,000. Both sides were provided *identical* information about the case and were asked what would be a fair settlement value. The plaintiff-respondents predicted an award nearly $18,000 higher than the defendant-respondents. George Lowenstein, et al., Self-Serving Assessments of Fairness and Pretrial Bargaining, 22 J. Legal Studies, 135 (1993).

c. *Equity-Seeking.* Even litigants and lawyers attempting to maximize their net-expected-outcomes in litigation may seek to accomplish non-monetary objectives, such as obtaining vindication from the other side or restoring fairness to a damaged relationship. See, e.g., Russell Korobkin & Chris Guthrie, *Psychological Barriers to Litigation Settlement: An Experimental Approach*, 93 Mich. L. Rev. 107, 144–47.

5.   Professor Korobkin writes "Reaching agreement for any amount that lies within the bargaining zone is superior to not reaching an agreement for both parties". Russell Korobkin, *A Positive Theory of Legal Negotiation*, 88 Georgetown L. Rev. 1789, 1792 (2000). And yet, researchers have found that negotiators regularly make irrational decisions and agree to terms that are past their reservation point and worse than their BATNA. Why might that be? Professor Leigh Thompson points to the agreement bias, the phenomenon of reaching a deal when there is no zone of potential agreement, or a negative bargaining zone. Leigh Thompson, THE MIND AND HEART OF THE NEGOTIATOR 214 (7th ed. 2020). This phenomenon is most prevalent when negotiators work alone and prioritize the social pressures of being liked or out of concern that others will perceive an impasse as a failure. When working within a team, negotiators are less prone to agreement bias because of the social pressures to be liked *within* the team as well as a greater information processing capacity. Leigh Taya R. Cohen, Geoffrey J. Leonardelli & Leigh Thompson, *Avoiding the Agreement Trap: Teams Facilitate Impasse in Negotiations with Negative Bargaining Zones*, 7 NEG. CONFLICT MGMT. RES. 232 (2014).

6.   Your reservation point can also help you determine whether to negotiate at all. Professors Deepak Malhotra and Max Bazerman give two examples in their book *Negotiation Genius*. The first and most straightforward is when your BATNA, and by extension your RP, beats your counterpart's best possible offer. This means there is no bargaining zone, and negotiating is simply wasting everyone's time. The second is when your counterpart knows that your BATNA, and by extension your RP, are weak in relation to an offer you have already received. With no comparable alternatives, making principled counteroffers is difficult, although not impossible.

DEEPAK MALHOTRA & MAX BAZERMAN, NEGOTIATION GENIUS: HOW TO OVERCOME OBSTACLES AND ACHIEVE BRILLIANT RESULTS AT THE BARGAINING TABLE AND BEYOND 285–86, 294–95 (2007).

7.   Negotiation goals or aspirations play an important part in negotiation preparation and in how people view their negotiation outcomes. Professor G. Richard Shell defines a negotiation goal as the "highest legitimate expectation of what you should achieve." BARGAINING FOR ADVANTAGE: NEGOTIATING STRATEGIES FOR REASONABLE PEOPLE 30 (2d ed. 2006). Offers based on hunches, feelings, or simple financial desires come across as unprincipled and undeserving of serious consideration. Andrea Kupfer Schneider, *Aspirations in Negotiation*, 87 Marq. L. Rev. 675, 678 (2004). What is it that makes an expectation legitimate?

8.   One benefit of goal setting is that it gives us a reference point that is more optimistic than one's reservation point. According to Shell:

> Researchers have discovered that humans have a limited capacity for maintaining focus in complex, stressful situations like negotiations. Consequently, once a negotiation is under way, we gravitate toward the single focal point that has the most psychological significance for us. Once most people set a firm bottom line in a negotiation, that becomes their dominant reference point as discussions proceed. They measure success or failure with reference to their bottom line.

G. RICHARD SHELL, BARGAINING FOR ADVANTAGE: NEGOTIATING STRATEGIES FOR REASONABLE PEOPLE 31 (2d ed. 2006).

Using the "reference point theory of aspirations," Professor Russell Korobkin tested the effects of various "settlement levers" associated with traditional litigation such as reservation points, perceptions of fairness, patience, and willingness to risk impasse. He concluded that while high aspirations help negotiators achieve more favorable bargaining results when a deal is reached, the associated cost was a higher risk of bargaining impasse and less overall satisfaction with bargaining outcomes. *Aspirations and Settlement*, 88 Cornell L. Rev. 1 (2002). *See also* Sally Blount White & Margaret A. Neale, *The Role of Negotiator Aspirations and Settlement Expectancies in Bargaining Outcomes*, 57 Org. Behav. & Human Decision Processes, 303, 305–307 (1994).

9.   Professor Clark Freshman and Dean Chris Guthrie also observe that while setting higher goals results in better objective results, it can also make negotiators feel worse about their negotiation outcomes. The reason is simple. Negotiators who set ambitious

Digging Deeper

How should a city compensate the wrongly imprisoned? http://www.npr.org/2016/07/27/487665663/how-does-a-city-compensate-the-wrongly-imprisoned-and-tortured.

goals routinely fall short of their aspirations. Freshman and Guthrie labeled this phenomenon the "goal-setting paradox" because "negotiators want both good results (objective success) and to feel good (subjective success)," objectives that can be in tension. To overcome the goal-setting paradox, Freshman and Guthrie suggest employing what they call the maximize-and-expand approach. To do this, negotiators should seek to expand their self-awareness by noticing their feelings and thoughts after a negotiation, expanding their self-acceptance by recognizing that substantial compliance with a goal may still be a good outcome, and focus on a broader scope of potential negotiation experiences and outcomes before, during, and after the negotiation. Clark Freshman & Chris Guthrie, *Managing the Goal-Setting Paradox: How to Get Better Results from High Goals and Be Happy*, 25 Negot. J. 217 (2009).

10. To counteract the psychological consequences noted above with respect to goal setting, a negotiator might set multiple goals along a continuum: Aspiration, Target, and Reservation. Using this approach, a negotiator uses objective criteria or another grounded principle to set each of these parameters. The negotiator's aspiration is the best legitimate outcome possible. Note that this aspiration may serve as a negotiator's first offer. A target is where the negotiator hopes to end up in the negotiation, and the reservation defines the point at which the negotiator's BATNA provides a better alternative.

11. As negotiators focus on their goals and aspirations, they move their focus from creating value to claiming value. This move can be easy or difficult depending on the interests at stake. For example, how do negotiators quantify abstract concepts like love, respect, goodwill, and the value of a human life?

2. Options

Well-prepared negotiators consider both their interests and their counterpart's interests and look for various options that may satisfy them. This analysis assists with value creation by increasing the likelihood that there will be mutually attractive options from which the negotiators can choose. Consider the following excerpt from Professor Menkel-Meadow.

CARRIE MENKEL-MEADOW, AHA? IS CREATIVITY POSSIBLE IN LEGAL PROBLEM SOLVING AND TEACHING IN LEGAL EDUCATION?
6 Harv. Negot. L. Rev. 97, 109–11 (2001)

One can structure a problem solving approach to negotiation by focusing on a three step process in which first, the lawyer identifies multiple classes of needs, objectives, interests or goals from one's own client. Then, s/he proceeds to do the same for other parties involved, using information available from public knowledge, research, client knowledge and from the negotiation session. Finally, the negotiator examines and matches loci of complementary and then conflicting needs and interests of the parties, in a systematic way, in order to craft solutions that maximize joint gain or Pareto-optimal solutions. . . .

* * *

Often a solution to a negotiated problem may be illuminated by exploring the characteristics of the "problem" mapped over parties' particular needs and interests. WHAT is the problem about? (What is the res? What is at stake? Can the thing itself be altered in any way?) WHO is involved? Are there stakeholders other than the parties formally at the table? Does adding parties facilitate a solution, or, as in the case of bringing in an insurer, does one increase those who can contribute to a solution, or, as in the case of the IRS, which is always a party to a legal negotiation, do tax concerns change the dynamics and suggest other solutions? WHERE is the transaction/ dispute/res located? Does jurisdiction matter for the problem? What about the location is alterable? (e.g., employment disputes with multiple offices or government agencies can offer transfer opportunities). WHEN does the dispute or transaction have to be resolved? This factor has led to the important and structural solutions of annuity payments in tort cases, installment payment contracts, contingency pricing and risk allocations, as well as continuing options, accelerated or graduated payments and duties and a whole host of substantive time-based solutions for trials, contingencies and terminable-upon-conditions arrangements. HOW may the matter be negotiated? Must solutions be conventional payments of money? Are other more creative solutions possible? In-kind trades? Apologies? Percentage of gross or net, instead of fixed sums? Contingent agreements? Secured obligations? Guarantors? Third party reviews? Can dispute resolution procedures themselves be altered? These framing questions for legal solutions to negotiated problems are a way of increasing the resources available for solving problems and probing for non-obvious solutions.

POINTS FOR DISCUSSION

1. Professor Menkel-Meadow mentions "Pareto-optimal" solutions. A "Pareto-superior" outcome is one that "makes at least one person better off and no one worse off." RICHARD A. POSNER, ECONOMIC ANALYSIS OF LAW 14–15 (5th ed. 1998). A solution is said to be Pareto-optimal when no other outcome improvements can be made. Alexander D. Northover, *"Enough and as Good" in the Intellectual Commons: A Lockean Theory of Copyright and the Merger Doctrine*, 65 EMORY L.J. 1363, 1383 n.138 (2016).

2.   Professor Leigh Thompson distinguishes options based on the amount of potential value created. Options of the first type are those that are within the distributive bargaining range. Options of the next or second level are those that are clearly better than those in the distributive bargaining range. And options of the final and third value level is those that reach the pareto-frontier. She says, "ideally, negotiators should always strive to reach level 3 integrative agreements. Higher levels are progressively more difficult for negotiators to achieve, but they are more beneficial to negotiators." Leigh Thompson, THE MIND AND HEART OF THE NEGOTIATOR, 47–48 (1st ed. 1998).

3.   Contingent agreements are a helpful creative tool that provides a means for "genuinely held disagreements about the future" to generate "an important opportunity for negotiators to discover an attractive exchange." Michael L. Moffitt, *Contingent Agreements*, *in* 1 THE NEGOTIATOR'S DESK REFERENCE 619 (Andrea Kupfer Schneider & Christopher Honeyman eds., 2017). Can you see a contingent agreement being viable to someone who is notably risk averse?

4.   One way that negotiators using the value-creating strategy can generate options is through brainstorming. In this process, negotiators generate as many options as possible, without judging them. Should parties brainstorm prior to negotiation as a way of preparing for the negotiation? What are the advantages and drawbacks of an option-generation process like brainstorming?

5.   Do you see any potential drawbacks to generating options? Dean Chris Guthrie suggests that the addition of options can give rise to four phenomena that tend to occur in the following order: devaluation of the initial option, inability to make decisions independent of context, indecision in choosing between options, and regret over the decision. Thus, negotiators who "generate multiple options may be induced by the very availability of those options to make decisions that run contrary to their true preferences and that induce negative post-decision emotions." Chris Guthrie, *Panacea or Pandora's Box? The Costs of Options in Negotiation*, 88 Iowa L. Rev. 601, 607–08 (2003). Multiple alternatives can also distort negotiators' assessment of the bargaining range. Michael Schaerer, David D. Loschelder & Roderick I. Swaab, *Bargaining Zone Distortions in Negotiations: The Elusive Power of Multiple Alternatives*, 137 Org. Behav. & Hum. Decision Processes 156 (2016).

3. Information Gathering

It is regularly said that information is power, and implicit in the discussions throughout this book is the idea that a negotiator, to be effective, has to gather information. A negotiator must gather information before the negotiation in order to have a good grasp on fundamental negotiation concepts such as interests, objective criteria, and BATNA. Without this information, a negotiator is likely to reach a sub-optimal deal because it will be nearly impossible to determine clear negotiation goals. Thus, negotiators should do as much investigation into the subject matter of the negotiation— fundamental negotiation concepts (interests, objective criteria, and BATNA), potential outcomes and options, and even one's negotiation counterpart—as possible. The more investigation that can be done before the negotiation, the better. Remember that you can use questions to do more than identify useful facts. Well-crafted questions, delivered well and with appropriate active listening, can help you to understand the other party's interests, available resources, and perceptions of available alternative options if they do not reach an agreement with you. Gaps in the available information form the basis for questions to ask the negotiation counterpoint as part of the information exchange phase of negotiation as discussed below.

> **Negotiation Nugget**
>
> One of the foundations of litigation practice is fact investigation, a skill woefully underdeveloped in legal education. The more you can develop these skills the better litigator and negotiator you will become.

4. Emotions

Many negotiation texts and articles gloss over the emotional component of negotiation for several reasons—emotions can be unpredictable and "messy," and more analytical people (like lawyers) tend to dismiss the power of emotions. Yet, negotiation is an inherently emotional activity, both for lawyers and clients. Negotiators' emotional responses to offers and counteroffers often result in negotiation errors. The next excerpt discusses how negotiators can understand and manage emotions by focusing on the five core concerns that lead to both positive and negative emotions.

LEONARD L. RISKIN, FURTHER BEYOND REASON: EMOTIONS, THE
CORE CONCERNS, AND MINDFULNESS IN NEGOTIATION

10 Nev. L.J. 289, 294–95, and 299 (2010)

* * *

I.   The Problem: Emotions in Negotiation

Most of us have trouble dealing with emotions that are associated with conflict. Negotiators—especially those trained in law—commonly address this problem by trying to exclude emotions from negotiation and to focus solely on so-called objective, rational factors, such as money. Negotiators may come to this approach through mentoring, training, or education. Most traditional law school courses, for instance, exclude consideration of the emotions of the parties, lawyers, and judges. But many negotiators adopt this approach without any training, and without even thinking about it. Some of them have little or no conscious awareness of emotions. Others may ignore emotions in order to avoid uncomfortable anxiety. Still others might fear that recognizing, expressing, or attempting to address emotions will overwhelm their cognitive faculties and escalate the conflict, making it more difficult to resolve.

Speaking generally, Fisher and Shapiro assert that the Core Concerns System can promote better interest-based negotiation by addressing some causes of negative emotions and fostering positive emotions. . . .

Although a negotiation that excludes direct expression or consideration of emotions often enables parties to settle disputes, it also can precipitate several problems. For instance, parties frequently will not reach the best feasible resolution because they fail to look beneath their asserted positions for the interests, beliefs and perspectives that lie beneath them. As Bernard Mayer has suggested, "full" resolution of a conflict requires resolution along three dimensions—cognitive, emotional, and behavioral. And, as Daniel Shapiro argues elsewhere, "[e]motions are a means to communicate relational identity concerns." Thus, to the extent that negotiators keep emotions out of the negotiation process, they—or their principals—are less likely to achieve an emotional resolution because they do not address the needs associated with such emotions. Of course, emotions tend to sneak in anyway. When that happens, these emotions can prompt adversarial perspectives and behavior, making it less likely that the substantive interests will get attention. In addition, negative emotions can impair the parties' ability to think clearly, render them vulnerable to exploitation, and possibly harm relationships.

Thus, negative emotions can even impair a negotiator's ability to skillfully conduct adversarial negotiations.

* * *

II.   Addressing the Challenge of Emotions in Negotiation: The Core Concerns System

In a negotiation, Fisher and Shapiro tell us, everyone has five "core concerns": appreciation, affiliation, autonomy, status, and role. We all want to feel appreciated by others, to affiliate with others, to have autonomy, to have others recognize our status, and to have a meaningful role. We have these concerns not only in negotiation, but also in many other interactions. . . .

Left unsatisfied, any of the core concerns can produce negative emotions. And negative emotions can interfere with good interest-based problem solving. Satisfaction of these core concerns, however, leads to positive emotions, and positive emotions enhance one's ability to engage skillfully in interest-based negotiation. Fisher and Shapiro believe that negotiators are influenced by too many emotions to notice and address directly; for that reason, they suggest that a more practical, robust approach is to deal with these emotions indirectly by employing the core concerns as a diagnostic "lens" (to understand the situation and to plan, conduct, and review the negotiation) and as a "lever" (to improve the situation by fostering positive emotions in all parties, which can support better interest-based negotiation). . . .

―――――――――

POINTS FOR DISCUSSION

1.   In their book, BEYOND REASON: USING EMOTIONS AS YOU NEGOTIATE (2005), Professors Roger Fisher and Daniel Shapiro state:

> These five core concerns [appreciation, affiliation, autonomy, status, and role] are not completely distinct from one another. They blend, mix, and merge. But each has its own special contribution in stimulating emotions. Together, these concerns more fully describe the emotional content of a negotiation than could any single core concern. The core concerns are analogous to the instruments a quintet uses to play Mozart's Woodwind Quintet. No sharp edges divide the contribution of the flute, oboe, clarinet, bassoon, and French horn. But together, the five instruments more fully capture the tone and rhythm of the music than could any individual instrument.

Id., at 18 (2005). If the five core concerns blend together, what does a negotiator do to best address the various blends of core concerns that present themselves?

2.   Emotions are a part of the human condition. When talking about emotions and negotiation, most negotiators focus on the negative emotions. In particular, anger and fear are often viewed as counterproductive to the negotiation process. Directing anger toward circumstances rather than at individuals is one way to keep anger from causing problems. Similarly, cooling off periods to release steam and regain composure can help negotiators manage anger in the moment. Preparation may be the best strategy for defusing fear. Another strategy for dealing with fear is acting confident, despite being fearful. While managing one's and one's client's emotions is difficult enough, managing a counterpart's emotions can be particularly difficult. The first step is keeping yourself apprised of the other's mood in order to defuse any issues before they arise. If that is not possible, typical strategies include refraining from matching the emotion, taking a break, and finding ways to help the other to save face. See generally Robert S. Adler, Benson Rosen & Eliot M. Silverstein, *Emotions in Negotiation: How to Manage Fear and Anger*, 14 Negot. J. 161 (1998); Allison Wood Brooks & Maurice E. Schweitzer, *Can Nervous Nelly Negotiate? How Anxiety Causes Negotiators to Make Low First Offers, Exit Early, and Earn Less Profit*, 115 Org. Behav. & Hum. Decision Processes 43 (2011).

Negotiation Nugget

Some negotiators try to fake anger as a negotiation strategy. People who display fake anger usually dissipate the anger very easily compared to those who are truly angry. Additionally, negotiators typically make greater demands when they believe that someone is using anger simply as a negotiation tactic. See Stephane Cote, et al., 49 J. Experimental Soc. Psych. 453 (2013).

3.   Another framework from which to consider emotions is the evolutionary theory of emotions. Evolutionary emotion theorists have identified two purposes for anger. First, anger serves to stop ongoing transgressions and deter future transgressions by the transgressor and, potentially, others. Second, anger arises when others place insufficient weight on the actor's welfare compared to their own welfare. When anger is activated in this way, the actor typically uses one of two tactics—inflicting costs (e.g., aggression) or withdrawing benefits—that are designed to recalibrate the other's lack of concern. See Keelah Williams & Art Hinshaw, *Outbursts: An Evolutionary Approach to Emotions in the Mediation Context*, 34 Negot. J. 164 (2018).

4.   A recent study by Professors Hajo Adam & Jeanne Brett examined the effects of anger in negotiations. They found that the targets of anger respond differently depending on whether the negotiation setting is cooperative—one where

people experience high levels of trust, benevolence, and the motivation to work together—or competitive—one where people experience high levels of distrust, selfish and defensive desires, and the motivation to engage in strategic behavior—or balanced between the two. In both cooperative and competitive settings, expressions of anger elicited hostile reactions—such as decreased interpersonal liking, reciprocal anger, or the desire to retaliate—that resulted in fewer concessions. However, in balanced settings, expressions of anger led targets to make "strategic inferences," hypothesizing about the expresser's toughness and intentions. Targets of anger then used this information to assess whether there was a real threat of impasse or escalation that required behavioral adjustments. As a result, the expression of anger in balanced settings led targets of anger to make greater concessions. See Hajo Adam & Jeanne Brett, *Context Matters: The Social Effects of Anger in Balanced, Cooperative, and Competitive Negotiation Situations*, 61 J. Experimental Soc. Psychology 44 (2015).

B. INFORMATION EXCHANGE

Negotiation Nugget

Research has shown that taking the time to build rapport and engage in small talk prior to conducting a negotiation via email increases the likelihood of reaching an agreement. Janice Nadler, *How Small Talk Can Facilitate E-mail Dealmaking*, 9 Harv. Neg. L.J. 223 (2004).

As you have likely deduced, much of negotiation is an exercise in gathering and distributing information to facilitate the discovery and disclosure of interests. While negotiators gather as much information as possible in their preparation, they cannot learn everything beforehand due to time, costs, availability, and other factors. This means that information gathering continues into the across-the-table stages of negotiation. Not only is the exchange of information the primary means of creating value, it also helps set the interpersonal relationship of the negotiators. Many negotiations flounder in this stage because of a lack of planning.

When information is a tradable commodity, its highest and best use is to create value. Thus, the basic goal in developing an information bargaining strategy is simply to determine what information is needed and how to get it, what information can be shared, and how to best protect the information that cannot be shared. In the subsections that follow, we discuss these topics in detail.

POINTS FOR DISCUSSION

1.   When creating an information exchange strategy, negotiators will feel the push and pull of the Negotiator's Dilemma. Negotiators should plan disclosure with an eye to reciprocity. Reciprocal disclosures should beget further disclosures of information. If one's disclosures are not being reciprocated, negotiators should be prepared to engage in more direct information gathering strategies. If these strategies are fruitless, negotiators should reassess their interests in pursuing a deal.

2.   When it comes to preparing an information exchange strategy, Director Grande Lum suggests the following approach:

In preparation for any negotiation use the three G's of information exchange: get, give, guard. First what information do you want to get or ask about? What facts of the situation do you want to know more about? . . . [W]hat more do you want to find out about the other party's interests? . . . Remember, that questions can propel a negotiation forward in ways that statements or arguments cannot.

Then, consider what information you want to *give* or share. The other side can often not meet your needs if it does not know what they are or if it does not know what is important to you. What do you want to disclose factually that will move the negotiation forward? What do you want to disclose that will help the other side feel more comfortable? What information do you want to share that reveals your strength or firmness? . . .

> **Negotiation Nugget**
>
> A study of English labor and contract negotiations in the late 1970s found that skilled negotiators asked twice the number of questions during negotiations than average negotiators, findings which have been confirmed across several disciplines. Such negotiators are likely to be better able to diagnose the possibilities for a deal, and also to have fewer misunderstandings and disagreements in the commitment and implementation stages. See, Neil Rackham and John Carlisle, *The Effective Negotiator—Part I: The Behavior of Successful Negotiators*, 2 J. of European Indus. Tr. 6 (1978).

The last category to prepare for is whether to guard or protect information. Certain information may convey desperation or urgency, and revealing it will give the other side an unnecessary advantage. If I am negotiating to sell a vacation condominium, I would guard the fact that I am in desperate need of money to pay off a personal debt.

GRANDE LUM, THE NEGOTIATOR'S FIELDBOOK: SIMPLE STRATEGIES TO HELP YOU NEGOTIATE EVERYTHING 110 (2d ed. 2011).

1.   Seeking Information

In an earlier excerpt Professor Fischer and Mssrs. Ury and Patton suggest that the two most important questions for gathering information are "why" and "why not." We agree. Director Lum offers two distinct and more specific strategies for seeking information when negotiating. One strategy is to start with general open-ended questions about needs, concerns, and desires followed up with specific questions to demonstrate listening as well as to move the conversation forward. He then advises following up with reflective questions to confirm understanding. The second strategy is to ask "challenge" questions about the value on the table. Challenge questions include the justification questions why and why not that Fisher, Patton, and Ury suggest, as well as questions about the problems and opportunities the other side faces. Lum advises following up with questions about the positive and negative consequences that might occur as a result of those problems and opportunities. Lum believes that challenge and consequence questions help create more value because they help discover the interests underlying a counterpart's positions. *See* GRANDE LUM, THE NEGOTIATOR'S FIELDBOOK: SIMPLE STRATEGIES TO HELP YOU NEGOTIATE EVERYTHING, 93–94 (2nd ed. 2011).

POINTS FOR DISCUSSION

1.   There are two steps to gathering information—identification and collection. When identifying information to gather, the first focus should be on the information that will help with creating value, typically things categorized as preferences. What information will help confirm, identify, or lead to discovering a counterpart's needs and interests? Next, the focus is on other information gaps, typically facts. Is there any other missing information that can help develop options, refine a BATNA, or assist in any other way? Finally, the phrase "missing information" does not refer just to holes in information, but also substitutes for information—presumptions, assumptions, and hypotheses—that have been used to assist with pre-negotiation planning.

2.   Professor Alexandra Carter suggests using the phrase "tell me . . ." as it allows the counterpart to fill in the relevant information. Specifically, she says:

> This question invites the other person to share with you (1) their view of the goal or problem that's brought you together; (2) any important

details relating to the problem or goal; (3) their feelings and concerns; (4) anything else they feel like adding. It's the negotiation equivalent of casting a giant net into the water to see how much you can catch. This question is the most important question you should use, for any negotiation, with any person, anywhere.

ALEXANDRA CARTER, ASK FOR MORE: 10 QUESTIONS TO NEGOTIATE ANYTHING, 127 (2020). Additionally, she believes that "tell me" invites a counterpart into a conversational partnership that encourages trust and openness. *Id.* at 131.

3.   Do you think that "challenge" questions might be off-putting to one's counterpart? If asked in the wrong way, they may put your counterpart on the defensive and result in less information received. The adage "it's not what you say, but how you say it," comes to mind. An exploratory, inquisitive, sincere, and non-accusatory tone is likely to be well received. The importance of tone becomes magnified when communicating via email and text messaging. What considerations should one take into account when negotiating on those communication platforms?

4.   How can the question "why" facilitate information-gathering about interests? Consider this example. In late 2000, the U.S. ambassador to the United Nations, Richard Holbrooke, was faced with a difficult task. The U.S. was more than $1 billion in arrears to the U.N. but was unwilling to pay unless the U.N. agreed to a number of reforms including reducing the U.S. contribution to the U.N. from 25% to 22% of the U.N.'s budget. With a hard deadline looming, Holbrooke's team changed tactics. Rather than focusing on persuasion, they focused on understanding why other nations would not contribute more to cover the 3% difference. Soon his team found that countries that might otherwise agree to increase their contributions did not have room to do so in their 2001 budgets, because they had already been finalized. Holbrooke then revised his proposal: immediately reduce U.S. assessments from 25% to 22% to meet Congress's deadline but delay the increase in contributions from other nations until 2002. Once the negotiators broadened their focus to include the issue of the timing, they could strike a deal that allowed each side to get what it wanted on the issue it cared about most. For more information about this negotiation, *see* Deepak Malhotra & Max H. Bazerman, *Investigative Negotiation*, Harv. Bus. Rev. 73–75 (Sept. 2007).

> **Negotiation Nugget**
>
> Negotiation has not traditionally been thought of as a persuasive activity, but it contains several theoretical components of persuasion—appeals to logic, appeals to emotion, and the speaker's character and credibility.

5.   Professor Ava J. Abramowitz instructs that asking questions serves several separate purposes. First, questions help us persuade others. Questions force others to think more deeply about the issue as they arrive at answers to questions.

Second, questions help to reveal a counterpart's needs, values, and priorities—crucial value creation material that determines whether a deal is possible. Questions also let you control the negotiation as you probe, confirm, clarify, and summarize. And finally, questions help expose problems in our own thinking, and since asking a question is not the same as putting forth an idea or suggestion, questions can also mask errors in your thinking. AVA J. ABRAMOWITZ, ARCHITECT'S ESSENTIALS OF NEGOTIATION 184–88 (2d ed. 2009).

6. Another method for eliciting information about a counterpart's interests is to make multiple equivalent simultaneous offers. Professors Jean R. Sternlight and Jennifer K. Robbennolt describe the method as follows:

> Offering multiple proposals for consideration at the same time can also be useful for gaining perspective on a negotiation counterpart's preferences. . . . By devising multiple proposals that are all equally acceptable to the client but that differ in subtle or not so-subtle ways, the attorney can gain information about the relative importance of different issues to the other side. Even if none of the proposals is acceptable to the other side, obtaining reactions to different alternatives can provide a great deal of insight that will be useful as additional proposals are created.

JEAN R. STERNLIGHT & JENNIFER K. ROBBENNOLT, PSYCHOLOGY FOR LAWYERS: UNDERSTANDING THE HUMAN FACTORS IN NEGOTIATION, LITIGATION, AND DECISION MAKING 262 (2012).

7. The other side of the question-asking coin is listening, which we discussed in more depth in Chapter One. Professor Charles B. Craver gives some practical tips about listening while in the heat of the information exchange.

> Skilled negotiators actively listen and carefully observe [counterparts] during the Information Stage. They maintain supportive eye contact to encourage further . . . disclosures and to discern verbal leaks and nonverbal clues. They use smiles and occasional head nods to encourage additional responses from adversaries who feel they are being heard. Active listeners not only hear what is being said, but recognize what is not being discussed, since they understand that omitted topics may suggest weaknesses [counterparts] do not wish to address.

Negotiation Nugget

Listening is an important skill when interviewing, negotiating, and eliciting witness testimony. Too many times, young attorneys are so focused on the questions that they have prepared that they fail to listen to the answers. Don't let that be you.

Questioners should listen carefully for [word choices] that inadvertently disclose important valuation information. For example [one] might say: "**I have to have** Item A, **I really want** Item B, and I would **like to get** Item C." Item A is **essential**—she has to have it. Item B is **important**—she really wants it, but does not have to have it. Item C is **desirable**—she would like to get it, but would be willing to give it up for anything better. These [expressions] disclose the true priorities of the items being discussed.

Advocates should proceed slowly during the Information Stage, because it takes time for the persons being questioned to decide what should be disclosed and when it should be divulged. Patient questioning and active listening are usually rewarded with the attainment of greater knowledge. Too many negotiators rush through the Information Stage, because they can hardly wait to begin the distributive portion of interactions. When impatient bargainers conduct an abbreviated Information Stage, they usually miss important pieces of information and achieve agreements that are less beneficial than the accords they might have obtained through a more deliberate questioning process.

CHARLES B. CRAVER, SKILLS AND VALUES: LEGAL NEGOTIATING 31 (2d ed. 2012) (emphasis in original).

8.   To be a good negotiator, it helps to be curious. Dean Chris Guthrie asks whether someone who "isn't naturally curious about her counterpart [can] become that way?" Focusing on "situational" curiosity, which is triggered by a particular activity or transaction, Dean Guthrie suggests the following curiosity-enhancing strategies: 1) set "listening goals, because researchers have found that people are more likely to be curious if they are trying to meet a challenge or goal"; 2) remember why it is helpful to listen "because researchers have found that people are more likely to remain interested in a task when they focus on the purposes served by performing it"; and 3) vary the means used to elicit information "because researchers have found that people are more likely to remain interested and engaged in a task if they vary the way they perform it." Chris Guthrie, *I'm Curious: Can We Teach Curiosity*, in RETHINKING NEGOTIATION TEACHING: INNOVATIONS FOR CONTEXT AND CULTURE 63, 65–67 (James Coben, Giuseppe De Palo & Christopher Honeyman eds., 2009). What "listening goals" would you set for yourself when negotiating?

9.   An underappreciated art of listening is noticing what is missing when people respond to questions. Professor Melissa L. Nelken advises:

Asking questions is only one way to gather information, and not always the most informative one. You also have to listen for what someone omits from an answer, for answers that are not answers or that deflect the question, for hesitations and vagueness in the responses that you get. There is no simple formula for what such things mean, but the more alert you are for ways in which you are not getting information in a straightforward way, the better able you will be to sort through the information that you get.

MELISSA L. NELKEN, NEGOTIATION THEORY AND PRACTICE 44 (2d ed. 2007).

2.   Sharing Information

Earlier we noted Director Lum's suggestion that when it comes to information sharing, negotiators should determine which information to "give and guard" as part of his "3 G's" information strategy. The following excerpt from Professor Menkel-Meadow provides a sound strategy for determining which information should be given and which should be guarded.

CARRIE MENKEL-MEADOW, KNOW WHEN TO SHOW YOUR HAND
Negot. Newsletter, June 2007, at 1, 1–3

Suppose that two entrepreneurs, a marketing expert and an IT specialist, are thinking about merging their consulting firms to create a greater synergy of services. As their talks unfold, each wonders how much information to disclose. Should they bring up discussions with other potential partners? When should they share proprietary business data? What if one is planning to retire in two years, and the other is starting a family—should they share this personal information?

* * *

In all your negotiations, you must calculate the risks and rewards of sharing information with your counterpart. Here, I will show you which factors to consider when making such decisions, when to ask for information directly, and when to seek it elsewhere.

A wealth of useful information

Before talks begin—and, if possible, even before your initial contact with your counterpart—list the information you need to resolve your dispute or to build a strong deal. Also anticipate the information the other side will want from you, and consider how you'll respond to these queries.

Information typically falls into these categories:

- Facts: Information about relevant past events, goods, and services; ongoing obligations and liabilities; parties needed to conclude talks; and so forth.

- Opinions, values, and predictions: Information subject to different interpretations, such as a company's value, the likely income from a new product, the outcome of a future court decision, or whether the dollar will rise or fall.

- Preferences: Information that negotiators express as their needs, interests, goals, objectives, desires, bottom lines, and reservation point.

Once you have identified the information you need and may be asked to reveal, you're ready to consider the reasons you and your counterpart might choose to disclose or to conceal it.

When to show your hand

For legal, ethical, and strategic reasons, you might choose to disclose these four types of information:

1.   Information required by law.

The last thing you want is for a good deal to be voided in post hoc legal proceedings. To fulfill legal standards (and your own code of ethics), research what you must disclose in a particular jurisdiction or realm of negotiation.

Pertinent laws include those on fraud and misrepresentation, disclosure law in securities and real estate, and consumer protection statutes. Mandatory disclosure rules can be national (such as the Sarbanes-Oxley Act), state, or local (such as those concerning hazardous-waste disposal).

In addition, ethics and disclosure rules apply to various professions. Lawyers and accountants may have to reveal adverse financial data and irregularities, real-estate brokers must reveal known defects in a property, and underwriters must disclose many conditions of a public offering.

2.   Information in the public domain.

Note

In Chapter 7, we point to the increasing availability of data to learn about and analyze historical judicial and lawyer behaviors.

In the age of Google searches and international networking, much information that was formerly hidden is now at our fingertips. Before deciding to conceal a piece of information, consider whether your counterpart is likely to discover it anyway. Here are some types of information to which the other side (and you, too!) may have access:

- Public information available on the Internet, including financial statements of public companies, disclosure statements for smaller companies and nonprofits, news reports, professional biographies, and lawsuit settlements.

- Proprietary information available from private investigators and sources who have dealt with you in the past.

- Information extracted through subpoenas, depositions, discovery, and other legal processes or made public through press leaks.

3.   Information that could inspire reciprocation.

In most negotiations, a pattern of reciprocity tends to develop. If you don't reveal key information, your counterpart may withhold in response. Failure to disclose can prevent you from getting the information you need.

Concealing information may be especially unwise when you're trying to build a relationship. Returning to the case of the two entrepreneurs, suppose that Mindy, the marketing expert, is trying to decide whether to reveal to Paul, the IT specialist, that she plans to retire in two years. Paul might view this information as a chance to grow the business on his own—or as a betrayal of the partnership. Hiding her plans not only could sour the relationship and the merger but also could damage Mindy's reputation in the industry and the community.

4.   Potentially damaging facts and needs.

It may sound counterintuitive, but sometimes you can benefit from revealing information that seems too risky to disclose. Consider how a trial lawyer might handle the possible revelation of damaging information about her client: by bringing it up during direct examination so as to minimize the odds of a disaster during cross-examination. Similarly, skillful negotiators choose to reveal and explain carefully information that might trouble the other side.

As social psychologist George Homans pointed out in the early 1960s, revealing preferences often illuminates complementary (rather than competing) goals and values. Mindy certainly would choose to disclose her impending retirement if she's looking for someone to carry on her business and suspects that Paul would love such an opportunity.

When to hold your cards

Now let's consider four types of information that may be best kept under wraps.

1. Sensitive or privileged information.

It can be tough to decide whether to disclose private or sensitive information, such as trade secrets and financial data, as well as your preferences (targets, reservation points, needs, and interests). This information is often necessary to identify tradeoffs and create value, but there's also the risk that your counterpart will take advantage of your disclosure. If Mindy reveals her retirement plans to Paul, he may try to bargain for a greater share of future profits.

* * *

2. Information that isn't yours to share.

When you negotiate as someone's agent—whether as a lawyer, a broker, or your firm's representative—disclosure decisions may not be yours to make. Instead, you'll first need to discuss the risks and benefits discussed here with your principal. Even if information doesn't technically "belong" to someone else, disclosure might hurt that person. Suppose you're negotiating a purchase from one supplier. You could be tempted to disclose another supplier's bottom line—but it might be wise to consult this party first.

3. Information that diminishes your power.

If you have less power than your counterpart, think through the potentially negative consequences of making "information concessions." Physically injured plaintiffs often are tempted to offer information about their current injuries in return for an early settlement, though they might procure greater damage awards later if longer-term injuries emerge. And in an overheated real-estate market, the bidder who expresses the greatest desire for a given house risks being exploited by a seller with multiple offers. Evaluate whether your desire for a given outcome might cause you to reveal too much and be exploited.

4. Information that may fluctuate.

"Facts" may change over time; prices and preferences certainly will. When important information seems unstable, you might choose to wait to reveal it or else seek a deal provision to later modify the information you share. Contractual contingencies allow you and your counterpart to "bet" on your differing predictions; you also can add clauses that permit renegotiation should facts or conditions change. Mindy and Paul might decide that if their joint company nets a certain profit in several years, she will take a percentage as retirement income but put off retirement if this goal is not realized.

POINTS FOR DISCUSSION

1.   There is widespread agreement among those who favor the value-creating approach to negotiation that negotiators need clear communication to help develop as wide a range of potential options as possible. Accentuating this point, Professor Menkel-Meadow has famously stated, "In short, there is no incentive to dissemble." Carrie Menkel-Meadow, *Toward Another View of Legal Negotiations: The Structure of Problem Solving*, 31 UCLA L. Rev. 754, 822 (1984). Research supports this conclusion, finding that disclosing one's priorities to a counterpart leads to better joint outcomes. See Simone Moran & Ilana Ritov, *Initial Perceptions in Negotiations: Evaluation and Response to "Logrolling" Offers*, 15 J. Behav. Decision Making 101 (2002); Ilana Ritov & Simone Moran, *Missed Opportunity for Creating Value in Negotiations: Reluctance to Making Integrative Gambit Offers*, 19 J. Behav. Decision Making 1 (2006). Consistent with the excerpt above, however, Menkel-Meadow also points out that blindly sharing information is ill advised.

> On the other hand, totally uninhibited information sharing may be as dysfunctional as withholding information. In experiential simulations Pruitt & Lewis found that there was not necessarily a correlation between free information exchange and joint profit. Instead, joint profit was associated with information processing—that is, the ability to listen to, receive, and understand the information and how it related concretely to the problem. Furthermore, information sharing in a thoughtless and unrestricted fashion may lead to the sharpening of conflict as value differences are revealed in competing goals and needs. In problem-solving negotiation, it is crucial to understand the usefulness and function of particular pieces of information—such as exploring how strongly one party desires something—because each piece is related to possible solutions. Problem solvers must determine what information is needed and why, and must be able to absorb information from the other side to test assumptions about needs, goals, and objectives.

Carrie Menkel-Meadow, *Toward Another View of Legal Negotiations: The Structure of Problem Solving*, 31 UCLA L. Rev. 754, 822–23 (1984).

2. When it comes to specifics, negotiators need to determine what kind of response is suitable for an open-ended question, and what is best suited for a direct question. If disclosure of certain information is anticipated but the time is not right, does one simply deflect the question by answering a question she would rather answer? Or does she signal some receptiveness and say, "let's get back to that in a moment" and delve into another topic? If a question aims directly at some information she wants to guard, how should she signal that the requested information is off limits without damaging the information exchange?

Negotiation Nugget

Open-ended questions are questions that cannot be answered with a simple "yes" or "no." Rather, they require one to provide a lengthier answer that helps provide insight as to what the responder believes to be important.

If a negotiator is being more strategic in disclosing information, there are several tactics, known as blocking techniques, that can help in avoiding the disclosure of strategic information. Such tactics include:

- changing the subject,

- delaying instead of answering immediately,

- answering a different question,

- responding with your own question,

- asking for clarification,

- discounting the question,

- answering a specific question by focusing on the general,

- answering the general by focusing on the specific, and

- answering only part of a question.

Digging Deeper

If these "blocking techniques" are shady, does that mean that they are unethical? Are any more disturbing than the others?

See MARTIN E. LATZ, GAIN THE EDGE! NEGOTIATING TO GET WHAT YOU WANT 64–66 (2004). Even though these techniques can seem somewhat shady, negotiators (and politicians) use them all the time. Those who use them need to be cognizant of protecting their credibility as well as their information. And, when collecting information, negotiators need to be on guard for these techniques and to keep asking probing questions when these techniques are being employed.

3.   The information exchange stage is also where negotiators evaluate their respective leverage. This brings forth an important point: Should negotiators reveal their BATNA's? According to Professor Shell,

> If you have attractive alternatives or good sources of normative leverage or can easily live without the other party's cooperation, the information exchange stage is the time to signal this to the other party. . . . You can either send a firm signal that you have the power to demand a favorable deal and intend to insist on one, or you can show your power and indicate you intend to be flexible in order to build goodwill for the future.

G. RICHARD SHELL, BARGAINING FOR ADVANTAGE: NEGOTIATION STRATEGIES FOR REASONABLE PEOPLE 152–53 (2d ed. 2006). And if your leverage is not so good? He advises one of two approaches. The first is to emphasize the inherent uncertainty of the future. The second is to simply acknowledge an obvious weakness. "[I]t may help both your credibility and your communication to personalize the situation as much as possible, arrange for a face-to-face meeting, candidly acknowledge the other side's power, and proceed on that basis." *Id.* at 153.

> **Digging Deeper**
>
> Rather than blocking, what if a negotiator lies in response? The issue of lying in a negotiation is covered in detail when we discuss negotiation ethics in Chapter 5.

> **Negotiation Nugget**
>
> Like BATNA, negotiators should carefully consider whether to disclose their reservation point in a negotiation. A good basic rule is to never disclose your reservation point unless you have exhausted all other options and are ready to walk away to your BATNA.

4.   BATNA disclosure is not a decision to be taken lightly. Director Lum advises that negotiators think through the consequences of disclosure.

What are the factors to consider in disclosure? Once your goal [to be accomplished through disclosure] is clear, you still have to take into account a number of factors before deciding whether or not to disclose your BATNA. Examine the ramifications disclosure will have on the negotiation itself and on the other party. Given these, will you be able to accomplish your goal, or will it get sidetracked? Sometimes, no matter how artfully you state your BATNA, sharing it is a declaration of war, so consider a worst-case scenario and . . . your ability to walk.

GRANDE LUM, THE NEGOTIATOR'S FIELDBOOK: SIMPLE STRATEGIES TO HELP
YOU NEGOTIATE EVERYTHING 107 (2d ed. 2011).

5.   Options serve an interesting and varied role as bridges from the
information exchange stage of negotiation to the offer and concession stage. When
working with an adversarial approach, options simply morph into traditional first
offers or a menu of proposals laid out to determine which to work upon. When
working with a value-creating mindset, options are not only developed as part of a
negotiator's preparation, they are also developed during the negotiation itself with
the assistance of one's counterpart to segue into the offer and concession stage. One
typical method of doing so is brainstorming. Participating in a brainstorming session
is difficult enough when everyone is working as a team, so how does one brainstorm
with a negotiation counterpart? Director Lum makes the following suggestions.

> Good negotiators create a comfortable atmosphere for discussing
> options. This is a core issue when it comes to brainstorming. . . .
> However, some people are so used to positional concessions-based
> negotiating that it is difficult to brainstorm. They will latch onto any idea
> that might suit them, or they are unwilling to create new options for fear
> of commitment. Be clear with each other that all ideas will be put on the
> table without commitment—that you will create value by investigating
> many possibilities.

> Another impediment to brainstorming is the fact that many people are
> more comfortable critiquing ideas then coming up with them—many are
> more accustomed to finding the one "right" answer from a list of choices.
> Articulate that the goal is to get ideas out there; evaluating will come later.

GRANDE LUM, THE NEGOTIATOR'S FIELDBOOK: SIMPLE STRATEGIES TO HELP
YOU NEGOTIATE EVERYTHING, 99 (2nd ed. 2011). Although difficult to do,
brainstorming can be a great way of uncovering interests as new options emerge.
And as negotiators enter the phase of deciding among a variety of options, they are
transitioning to the offer and concession stage, discussed in the following section.

6.   With the new information gleaned during the information exchange stage,
negotiators should take a moment to reassess their negotiation planning. How has
their understanding of their counterpart's interests, needs, BATNA, and any other
factors changed? With this information in mind, negotiators should assess whether
to alter strategies, objectives, and goals going forward.

C.   OFFERS AND CONCESSIONS

Offers and concessions are the means for claiming value in negotiations.
Thus, this stage is what most people imagine when they think of negotiation.
Effective negotiators take several factors into consideration during this stage,
including objective criteria, messaging, timing, BATNA, and reservation

points. Context matters as well. Understanding and planning how to maneuver through a negotiation's bargaining stage may be the most neglected aspect of thoughtful negotiation preparation.

1.   Standard Concession Practice

The following excerpt by Professor G. Richard Shell relays the sound conventional wisdom of offers and concessions. As you read, note that it discusses how different negotiation approaches manage offers and concessions.

G. RICHARD SHELL, BARGAINING FOR ADVANTAGE: NEGOTIATION STRATEGIES FOR REASONABLE PEOPLE
166–72 (2d ed. 2006)

When the stakes are all that matter, research shows that a firm concession strategy works best. In simple, price only negotiations . . . classic haggling is the rule: Open optimistically, hold for a bit, show a willingness to bargain, then make a series of progressively smaller concessions as you close in on your expectation level.

* * *

In more important, high-stakes deals, you should also be careful not to make big concessions too early. Start slowly. Why? Because big moves made early in bargaining can confuse the other side.

* * *

. . . When you make large concessions early in high-stakes transactional bargaining, you send a set of messages. One message is: *I really want this deal.* That message has leverage implications, and the other side may develop high expectations regarding the final price. It will want to test this hypothesis. . . .

The second message you send is: *The issues I conceded were not important to me.* . . . The other party may give you zero credit for this concession because you gave it up so easily.

* * *

If many issues are on the table, concession making in high-stakes negotiation often takes the form of "issue trading" instead of simple haggling. Negotiation scholars use the term "distributive bargaining" to describe simple haggling (people are "dividing the pie") and the term "integrative bargaining" to describe the more complex process of trading off between issues (people are "making the pie bigger" by matching or "integrating" their interests, priorities, and differences). Many deals contain both concession-making strategies.

How do classic hagglers handle a high-stakes negotiation with many different issues? Simple: They attack each issue one at a time and use the distributive procedure ... to reach their desired expectation level on each issue. They start high, concede slowly, and close on issue 1. Then they repeat the process on issue 2. And so on.

* * *

How does one engage in integrative bargaining? By identifying the issues, fears, and risks that are most important to each side and then "logrolling"—accommodating each other's most important interests and priorities in exchange for reciprocal accommodations.

... [T]he rule of thumb for integrative bargaining is to *make big moves on your "little" (less important) issues and little moves on your "big" (most important) issues.*

* * *

After a discussion of all of the issues (without making any concrete opening offers on any of them), issue trading often proceeds through "package bargaining." One side proposes a total package, including a demand on each issue. The other side responds with a total package of its own, reflecting its aspirations. Up to this point, the procedure looks just like haggling, but it changes after the openings.

In their next move, the side that opened may make concessions on one or two of its "little" issues, making a display of its sacrifices, but hold firm on its more important priorities. The other side reciprocates, and after several rounds each side begins to figure out which issues are more important to the other.

By dealing with entire packages and agreeing that no issue is closed until all issues have been decided, both parties retain a high degree of flexibility. If, later in the process, they find themselves at an impasse over an issue considered vital (such as price), they have the option of going back to earlier packages and exploring different combinations without being locked into any particular concession on any particular issue.

Parties often trade issues in clusters, using a formulation well known to negotiation experts: *IF you give us what we want on issues A and B, THEN we might consider concessions on issues X and Y.* The "if ... then" formula ensures that you never make a concession without linking it to a mutual concession from the other party. . . . The parties may eventually need to haggle and fight over some of the issues that both think are important, but they have "issue-traded" on the ones that each can concede at a relatively low cost.

* * *

[W]here both the future relationship and the stakes are roughly equal in importance for both sides, a variety of different bargaining and problem-solving procedures work. The goal is to address as many priorities as possible, make sure that each side gets its "fair share" on issues such as price, and maintain good working relationships between the parties going forward.

Because the stakes matter, you should still come to the table with high expectations. You will want to move slowly on your least important issues first and use the conditional "if . . . then" formulation for concession making. All trades should be reciprocal.

Because the relationship matters to both sides, more imaginative kinds of bargaining tactics are both possible and desirable. . . . Aggressive, hardball moves and transparent gambits do not work well. They are too bruising to personal feelings and usually obscure the shared interests the parties bring to the table. Instead, each party needs to probe more deeply into the real needs underlying the other side's demands and seek imaginative solutions. . . .

* * *

Interest-based, problem-solving approaches to bargaining work well in [these] situation[s]. Why? Because they give parties a chance to "make the pie bigger" both within the context of the transaction at hand (by using integrative bargaining techniques) and the larger framework of the parties' ongoing relationship (by creatively exploiting their ability to help each other in the future).

POINTS FOR DISCUSSION

1.   The back-and-forth of typical offer and concession behavior rests upon the reciprocity norm identified by Professor Robert B. Cialdini in his important book INFLUENCE: SCIENCE AND PRACTICE (5th ed. 2009).

> The general rule says that a person who acts in a certain way toward us is entitled to a similar return action.

* * *

> The reciprocation rule brings about mutual concession in two ways. The first is obvious; it pressures the recipient of an already-made

concession to respond in kind. The second, while not so obvious, is pivotally important. Because of a recipient's obligation to reciprocate, people are freed to make the initial concession and, thereby, to begin the beneficial process of exchange. After all, if there were no social obligation to reciprocate a concession, who would want to make the first sacrifice? To do so would be to risk giving up something and getting nothing back. However, with the rule in effect, we can feel safe making the first sacrifice to our partner, who is obligated to offer a return sacrifice.

Because the rule for reciprocation governs the compromise process, it is possible to use an initial concession as part of a highly effective compliance technique. The technique is a simple one that we will call the rejection-then-retreat technique, although it is also known as the door-in-the-face technique. Suppose you want me to agree to a certain request. One way to increase the chances that I will comply is first to make a larger request of me, one that I will most likely turn down. Then, after I have refused, you make the smaller request that you were really interested in all along. Provided that you structured your requests skillfully, I should view your second request as a concession to me and should feel inclined to respond with a concession of my own—compliance with your second request.

Id. at 36–38.

To prove the power of the strategy, Professor Cialdini set up an experiment where two groups of volunteers would ask college students if they would be willing to serve as volunteer chaperones for a group of juvenile delinquents on a day trip to the zoo. One group made a straightforward request which 83% of the requests were refused. The other group first asked college students to act as counselors for juveniles for two hours a week over a two-year period. Only after the request was refused were they asked to chaperone the two-hour zoo trip. With this group the acceptance rate was 51%, a rate three times higher. Id. at 38–39.

2.   The concession tactic that Cialdini describes above entails offering a concession as a way to induce their counterparts to do the same. Making concessions is not so easy, however, and the two negotiators are not likely to value their respective concessions in the same way. Psychologists have found that individuals experience more pain from a loss than they experience pleasure from a gain of the same size— a phenomenon known as loss aversion. As applied to negotiation, one result can be concession aversion, in which a negotiator experiences his own concessions as "losses" from his prior position. He will see those concessions as being bigger than will his opponent, who experiences them as "gains." Making concessions is also complicated by "reactive devaluation." Research on this phenomenon suggests that negotiators may devalue proposals simply because they have been offered by their "opponent." For a discussion, see Richard Birke & Craig R. Fox, *Psychological Principles in Negotiating Civil Settlements*, 4 Harv. Negot. L. Rev. 1, 48–49 (1999).

3.   In addition to reciprocity, negotiators can use several other psychological techniques to persuade their counterparts to make valuable concessions:

- Liking—"People prefer to comply with requests made by those they know and like. People tend to like those who are physically attractive; those with whom they share something in common; those with whom they are familiar; and those who pay them compliments." Chris Guthrie, *Courting Compliance, in* THE NEGOTIATOR'S FIELDBOOK: A DESK REFERENCE FOR THE EXPERIENCED NEGOTIATOR 371, 372 (Andrea Kupfer Schneider & Christopher Honeyman eds., 2006).

- Social proof—People "view a behavior as correct in a given situation to the degree that we see others performing it." ROBERT B. CIALDINI, INFLUENCE: SCIENCE AND PRACTICE 99 (5th ed. 2009).

- Authority—"Individuals often feel an obligation to comply with those who are in real or perceived authority positions." Chris Guthrie, *Courting Compliance, in* THE NEGOTIATOR'S FIELDBOOK: A DESK REFERENCE FOR THE EXPERIENCED NEGOTIATOR 371, 374 (Andrea Kupfer Schneider & Christopher Honeyman eds., 2006).

- Scarcity—" '[O]pportunities seem more valuable to us when they are less available.' Scarcity induces compliance in large part because it threatens our freedom of choice ('If I don't act now, I will lose the opportunity to do so.')" *Id.* at 374 (quoting Cialdini).

4.   An underappreciated aspect of making offers and counteroffers is the messaging surrounding them. In an interesting study described by Deepak Malhotra and Max H. Bazerman, Professor Ellen Langer and her colleagues found that justifying one's requests can make a difference in whether others will accede to a request. As part of the study, they had every copy machine in their university's library but one shut down (this was long before the internet age). As you might imagine, the one remaining copy machine was in high demand.

> The researchers were interested in finding out what would convince people to let others cut in front of them. In some instances, a researcher simply said, "Excuse me, I have five pages. May I use the Xerox machine?" Sixty percent of those approached this way allowed the researcher to cut in front of them. Other people were approached with a slightly different request: "Excuse me, I have five pages. May I use the Xerox machine *because I have to make some copies?*" As you can see, the second approach added an entirely inane justification (obviously, the reason for wanting to cut in line at the copy machine is to make copies!). What was the response this time? Ninety-three percent of those

approached with this request allowed the researcher to cut in front of them!

DEEPAK MALHOTRA & MAX H. BAZERMAN, NEGOTIATION GENIUS: HOW TO OVERCOME OBSTACLES AND ACHIEVE BRILLIANT RESULTS AT THE BARGAINING TABLE AND BEYOND 167 (2007). The lesson we learn from this is that negotiators should always have a principled justification for any request made while negotiating. *See* Ellen Langer, Arthur Blank, and Benzion Chanowitz, *The Mindlessness of Ostensibly Thoughtful Action: The Role of "Placebic" Information in Interpersonal Interaction*, 36 J. Personality & Soc. Psych.635 (1978).

5.   Continuing with the theme of messaging, mediator J. Anderson Little believes the messaging around offers and counteroffers is often misunderstood. This is because many negotiators fail to make credible initial offers or initial counteroffers, thereby causing their counterparts to make reactionary counteroffers out of anger and frustration. As a result, their proposals do not convey clear and accurate messages about the boundaries of the negotiation's bargaining zone. J. ANDERSON LITTLE, MAKING MONEY TALK: HOW TO MEDIATE INSURED CLAIMS AND OTHER MONETARY DISPUTES 66–69 (2007).

To combat this problem, Martin E. Latz advises that the messaging accompanying offers be specific and detailed, focused first on rationales and standards before mentioning terms. Such offers, he suggests, are perceived as more thoughtful, reasoned, serious, and thorough. They increase the chances of getting a response that is equally detailed. And starting with rationales and standards helps demonstrate reasonability while decreasing interpersonal difficulties and the likelihood of quick impasse. As negotiators plan their concession moves, they should also practice the messaging surrounding their offers and concessions. MARTIN E. LATZ, GAIN THE EDGE: NEGOTIATING TO GET WHAT YOU WANT 183–85 (2004).

6.   Imagine that you are in a negotiation that you thought was going well. Opposing counsel then makes an outrageous demand, entirely outside any reasonable settlement range. You now know this negotiation will take much longer and be more difficult than you had anticipated—and you know your client will not be happy with this news or with you. How do you feel about opposing counsel now? Attribution theory is the study of how we interpret the actions of others. When another person's action hurts us, we search for the cause. Was the other person's action intentional or not? Was it caused by the person's disposition or the circumstance in which the person found herself? How much control did the person have over what happened? Interestingly, we tend to underestimate the extent to which people's behavior is influenced by the circumstances in which they find themselves. Instead, we tend to emphasize explanations that focus on the general disposition and intentions of the person. This is called the fundamental attribution error—fundamental because we all do it and error because empirical study establishes that situational influences have more sway than we are inclined to think. See Lee Ross, *The Intuitive Psychologist and His*

Shortcomings: Distortions in the Attribution Process?, in 10 ADVANCES IN EXPERIMENTAL SOCIAL PSYCHOLOGY 174, 184–87 (Leonard Berkowitz ed., 1977).

As an example, Professor Keith Allred notes: "[R]esearch indicates that in observing a person at an airport yelling at an airline agent, one tends to overattribute the behavior to bad temper and underattribute it to circumstances, such as having recently been the victim of recurring unfair treatment by the airline." Keith C. Allred, *Anger & Retaliation in Conflict: The Role of Attribution, in* THE HANDBOOK OF CONFLICT RESOLUTION: THEORY AND PRACTICE 237, 240–41 (Morton Deutsch, Peter T. Coleman & Eric C. Marcus eds., 2d ed. 2006). At the same time, we are more likely to take into account situational factors when making attributions about our own behavior than we are when we are thinking about other people—a phenomenon known as the actor-observer effect. Edward E. Jones & Richard E. Nisbett, *The Actor and the Observer: Divergent Perceptions of the Causes of Behavior, in* ATTRIBUTION: PERCEIVING THE CAUSES OF BEHAVIOR 82 (Edward E. Jones et al. eds., 1972).

7.   As every negotiation shifts into the offer and concession stage, someone must make the first offer. That is, someone must make the initial distributive proposal that could result in an agreement. The question plaguing negotiators, then, is whether they should make the first offer or allow or compel their counterpart to do so.

Based on a series of experiments investigating how first offers operate, Professor Adam D. Galinsky and his colleagues developed the Information-Anchoring Model of First Offers. This model posits that first offers can have two primary effects. First, first offers act as anchors that influence final outcomes. Second, first offers may convey information about the negotiator's central concerns and priorities. When a negotiation is purely distributive, the anchoring effect of the first offer tends to impart a first-mover advantage because the

> **Digging Deeper**
>
> A lot of people simply try to avoid making first offers. In addition to those identified by Professor Galinsky, what are the advantages and disadvantages to making first offers?

first offer sets an anchor. In integrative negotiations, however, the effects of first offers are more complex. The researchers found that when first offers were uninformative as to the negotiator's priorities, the anchoring effect dominated and the negotiator making the first offer claimed more value. On the other hand, when first offers disclosed information about priorities—for example, "issue x is really the most important part of this deal"—joint gains and integrative insights were greater, but less value was claimed by the negotiator who made the first offer. Characteristics of the negotiation counterpart also turned out to be relevant. Negotiators who made first offers claimed more value when their counterpart had a prosocial orientation. But more self-oriented counterparts leveraged the information revealed by the first offer to make low-cost concessions in exchange for larger shares of the negotiation's value. D.D. Loschelder, R. Trottschel, R.I. Swaab, M. Friese, & A.D. Galinsky, *The Information-Anchoring Model of First Offers: When Moving First Helps Versus Hurts Negotiators*, 101 J. Applied Psych. 995 (2016).

8.   If you are going to make a first offer, what should it be? Professors Malhotra and Bazerman advise: "You should never make an offer so extreme that it cannot be stated as follows: 'I would like to propose X, because . . .' If you cannot finish this sentence in any meaningful way, you are probably asking too much." DEEPAK MALHOTRA & MAX H. BAZERMAN, NEGOTIATION GENIUS: HOW TO OVERCOME OBSTACLES AND ACHIEVE BRILLIANT RESULTS AT THE BARGAINING TABLE AND BEYOND 35 (2007). Professor Shell recommends that if a negotiator has decided to open, she should offer "the highest (or lowest) number for which there is a supporting standard or argument enabling . . . a presentable case." G. RICHARD SHELL, BARGAINING FOR ADVANTAGE: NEGOTIATION STRATEGIES FOR REASONABLE PEOPLE 160 (2d ed. 2006).

> ### Negotiation Nugget
>
> When wondering who should make the first offer, the general rule is that sellers go first. Usually, it's easy to identify which party should be considered "the seller." For example, in litigation the plaintiff is considered the seller because s/he is selling a legal claim. But, when there are several cross-claims and counterclaims, determining the seller can be quite complicated.

This advice is borne out by research suggesting that negotiators who begin with optimistic and justifiable positions often fare quite well. According to Dan Orr and Dean Chris Guthrie:

Due to a phenomenon that psychologists call "anchoring," we are often unduly influenced by the initial figure we encounter when estimating the value of an item. This initial value serves as a kind of reference point or benchmark that anchors our expectations about the item's actual value.

Negotiation and dispute resolution scholars have observed that this phenomenon could have an impact on negotiation. In a number of studies, researchers have shown that opening offers and demands, insurance policy caps, statutory damage caps, negotiator aspirations, and other "first numbers" can influence negotiation outcomes in transactions and settlements. What no researcher has done, however, is assess how potent this phenomenon is.

* * *

Our meta-analysis demonstrates that anchoring has a powerful influence on negotiation outcomes. Across the studies in our sample, we find a correlation of 0.497 between the initial anchor and the outcome of the negotiation. . . .

In lay terms, the 0.497 correlation means that every one dollar increase in an opening offer is associated with an approximate fifty-cent increase in the final sale price. A simple conversion provides another estimate of the impact anchoring can have on a negotiation. The square of a correlation provides an estimate of the amount of variance that it explains. The r-squared value of the correlation in our study is 0.247. In general terms, this mean that nearly 25 percent of the difference in outcomes among negotiations can be accounted for as a function of an opening offer or other initial anchor. (This finding is consistent with other research showing that an opening offer and initial counteroffer account for 57.6 percent of the variance in negotiated outcomes.)

Dan Orr & Chris Guthrie, *Anchoring, Information Expertise, and Negotiation: New Insights from Meta-Analysis*, 21 Ohio St. J. on Disp. Resol. 597, 597–98, 621–22 (2006).

2. Creating Value Through Offers and Concessions

Consider the following advice for negotiators who want to use a value creation approach when negotiating a settlement in litigation.

ROBERT H. MNOOKIN, SCOTT R. PEPPET & ANDREW S. TULUMELLO, BEYOND WINNING: NEGOTIATING TO CREATE VALUE IN DEALS AND DISPUTES
240–42 (2000)

[W]e advise lawyers interested in moving to the interest-based table to deliver three explicit messages to their counterparts. First, looking for trades may be good for both sides. Moving to the interest-based table may strengthen the parties' relationship, facilitate value-creating deals, and ease distributive tensions at the net-expected-outcome table. Second, looking for trades does not require or imply a ceasefire. Litigation can continue, and a party need not disclose information at the interest-based table that he feels will undermine his position at the net-expected-outcome table. Finally, discussing interests does not signal weakness. Indeed, a willingness to broaden the scope of negotiations can be framed as a sign of strength and confidence.

Searching for Trades

If the other side is willing to try to convert your dispute into a deal, you must first negotiate a process. If you have thought carefully about the other side's interests and come up with options that meet those interests, you may be tempted to unveil all your ideas at once, as in: "I know what you really want, and I've got the solution that gives you what you want." This is a dangerous tendency, and it is unlikely to work. Even if you have guessed right about the other side's interests, he is likely to reject what you propose, either because he has not been given an opportunity to speak for himself or because of reactive devaluation.

Instead, jointly explore what each side cares about and why, and what each side hopes the lawsuit will accomplish. Think broadly—don't just include obvious interests related to the lawsuit, such as "settle quickly" or "receive fair compensation." Also consider interests beyond the scope of the litigation. If two businesses are involved, what are their general business interests? To sell more product? Attract more customers? Expand geographically? Specialize in some area? Reduce costs? What are the interests of the individuals who run those businesses? What synergies exist? Can one side provide the other side with goods or services in a mutually advantageous way? What differences exist between the parties in resources, capabilities, and preferences? How can they trade on those differences?

In some cases, the parties may have important interests beyond the dollar amount of damages at issue. A defendant in an employment discrimination suit may worry about its reputation. Plaintiffs bringing a civil rights complaint against a police department may be interested in an admission of wrongdoing and changing police practices and policies in the future. The seller in a long-term supply contract may have an interest in establishing a more flexible delivery schedule in order to respond to market changes.

Also consider involving clients more at the interest-based table than at the net-expected-outcome table. Of course, if an attorney is accustomed to negotiations that focus on assessing the net expected outcome of litigation, she may not be comfortable with having her clients play an active role at the bargaining table. Relinquishing control can be difficult. But as we have noted, clients often understand their interests and the relative priorities among those interests better than their lawyers do, and they can often be very helpful at the interest-based table.

Finally, consider involving nonparties in searching for trades. The tendency in legal dispute resolution is to focus only on those people or institutions that are named parties in the litigation and to forget that each side has many other relationships that may be affected by the lawsuit. Adding some of these players at the interest-based table can be helpful. If, for example, a building owner and a general contractor are having a dispute over payment, they might bring in an official from the lending institution underwriting the project to assist with their negotiation. If they find a value-creating trade that requires additional lending, this official will be indispensable to making their creative solution possible. Similarly, in a dispute among coauthors over copyright issues, it may be helpful to bring in a representative of the publisher. As the frame of the negotiation widens, outside parties may be essential to devising sophisticated trades.

POINTS FOR DISCUSSION

1.   Under what circumstances are lawyer-negotiators most likely to favor a value creation approach to settlement discussions? What difference might it make if the disputing clients expect to have an ongoing relationship? Will it matter whether the litigants are "one-shotters" or "repeat players" in litigation? What difference might the relationship between the attorneys make?

2.   How central should law be to the settlement process? Some believe that settlements should reflect what a court of law would decide; others believe that settlement should simply reflect the parties' preferences. Others, like lawyer-mediator Gary Friedman believe that law is relevant but that it should not be assumed to be determinative—i.e., that " 'the law' may point to relevant principles or values which the parties might want to consider in approaching their own resolution of the issues." GARY J. FRIEDMAN, CENTER FOR THE DEVELOPMENT OF MEDIATION IN LAW TRAINING MATERIALS, MEMO #6 (1983).

Reflecting this latter view at a more fundamental level, Professors Mnookin and Lewis Kornhauser say negotiators "bargain in the shadow of the law." Writing in the context of divorce negotiations, they state:

> **Digging Deeper**
>
> Is it fair to say that the law is a form of objective criteria discussed earlier in Chapter Two?

Divorcing parents do not bargain over the division of family wealth and custodial prerogatives in a vacuum; they bargain in the shadow of the law. The legal rules governing alimony, child support, marital property, and custody give each parent certain claims based on what each would get if the case went to trial. In other words, the outcome that the law will impose if no agreement is reached gives each parent certain bargaining chips—an endowment of sorts.

Robert H. Mnookin & Lewis Kornhauser, *Bargaining in the Shadow of the Law*, 88 Yale L. J. 950, 968 (1979).

3. Some commentators have argued that the mindset required for litigating a case to verdict is so different from the mindset required for settlement that clients might benefit from hiring special "settlement counsel." Indeed, some clients do retain counsel to play this sole role. See e.g., Jim Golden, H. Abigail Moy & Adam Lyons, *The Negotiation Counsel Model: An Empathetic Model for Settling Catastrophic Personal Injury Cases*, 13 Harv. Negot. L. Rev. 211 (2008).

3. Apologies

One issue that often comes up in dispute resolution is that of apologies. This makes sense given that negotiations surrounding litigation involve a sense of being wronged, and many people have a dignitarian interest in having this harm acknowledged. Indeed, it can be the most important issue to address, regardless of how the dispute actually presents itself.

> **Negotiation Nugget**
>
> For a more robust discussion of this research, see Jennifer K. Robbennolt, *Apologies and Legal Settlement: An Empirical Examination*, 102 Mich. L. Rev. 460 (2003).

Yet as most of us can probably appreciate from our personal experience, not all apologies are effective. In fact, some apologies can make the situation worse. So, for the negotiator who senses an apology may be appropriate, it is important to consider the nature of the apology and its value to the parties in reaching settlement. In the following excerpt, Professor Robbennolt reports on her empirical study of these questions.

JENNIFER K. ROBBENNOLT, APOLOGY—HELP OR HINDRANCE? AN EMPIRICAL ANALYSIS OF APOLOGIES' INFLUENCE ON SETTLEMENT DECISION MAKING
10 Disp. Resol. Mag. 33, 33–34 (2003–2004)

Recently, I conducted a series of experimental studies designed to begin a systematic examination of whether, in what ways and under what conditions apologies might affect settlement decisionmaking. The findings described here are based on the results of two experimental studies in which 506 participants were asked to read a vignette describing a pedestrian-bicycle accident, to take on the role of the injured party, to indicate whether or not they were likely to accept a settlement offer, and to respond to a series of questions about the situation.

All participants reviewed the same basic scenario and evaluated the same settlement offer. However, some participants evaluated a version of the scenario in which no apology was offered; a second group evaluated a version of the scenario in which the other party offered a partial apology that merely expressed sympathy for the potential claimant's injuries (i.e., 'I am so sorry that you were hurt.'); and a third group of participants evaluated a version of the scenario in which the other party offered a full apology that took responsibility for causing the injuries (i.e., 'I am so sorry that you were hurt. The accident was all my fault.'). Thus, the only difference between the three groups was the nature of the apology offered.

Apologies Affect Settlement

In the first study, even though all participants were told that they had suffered the same injuries and received the same offer of settlement, the nature of the apology offered influenced recipients' willingness to accept the offer. Receipt of a full, responsibility-accepting apology increased the likelihood that the offer would be accepted. In contrast, a partial, sympathy-expressing apology increased participants' uncertainty about whether or not to accept the offer.

Specifically, when no apology was offered, 52 percent of respondents indicated that they would definitely or probably accept the offer, while 43 percent would definitely or probably reject the offer, and 5 percent were unsure. When a partial apology was offered, only 35 percent of respondents were inclined to accept the offer, 25 percent were inclined to reject it and 40 percent indicated that they were unsure. In contrast, when a full apology was offered, 73 percent of respondents were inclined to accept the offer, with only 14 percent inclined to reject it and 14 percent unsure.

In addition, a full apology resulted in more positive ratings of numerous variables that are thought to underlie settlement decision making than did either a partial apology or no apology. Where there were differences in participants' responses across conditions, the differences follow a strikingly similar pattern: failing to offer an apology or offering a partial apology elicited equivalent responses on these measures that were both different from the responses elicited when a full apology was offered.

Thus, as compared to offenders who offered either a partial apology or no apology, an offender who offered a full apology was seen as:

- having offered a more sufficient apology
- experiencing more regret
- being more moral
- being more likely to be careful in the future
- believing that he or she was more responsible for the incident, and
- having behaved less badly.

In addition, participants who received a full apology, as opposed to a partial apology or no apology, expressed:

- greater sympathy for the offender
- less anger, and
- more willingness to forgive the offender.

Finally, participants who received a full apology, as opposed to a partial apology or no apology, anticipated:

- less damage to the parties' relationship, and
- that the settlement offer would better make up for their injuries.

These underlying judgments provided the mechanism by which apologies influenced settlement decisions. Beyond their effect on decisions regarding a particular offer, such judgments might also be expected to influence the willingness and ability of litigants to engage in settlement negotiations more generally.

POINTS FOR DISCUSSION

1.   While "full" apologies have the most consistently positive effects on disputant perceptions, simple expressions of sympathy can sometimes have beneficial effects as well. Statements that are not fully apologetic may be difficult to interpret and signals about the sincerity with which they are offered may be particularly important. See Jennifer K. Robbennolt, *Apologies and Settlement Levers*, 3. J. Empirical Studies 333 (2006). Think about how you might advise a client. Under what circumstances would you advise a client to apologize? Express sympathy?

2. Additional research has found that while attorneys understand the content of apologies in ways that are similar to the ways in which disputants understand them, attorneys are more attuned to the strategic value of apologies—that is, they are more likely to see the apology as an admission—than are disputants. See Jennifer K. Robbennolt, *Attorneys, Apologies, and Settlement Negotiation*, 13 Harv. Negot. L. Rev. 349 (2008). How might this different perspective influence the way in which an attorney might counsel a client? How might it affect negotiation with the other side?

> **Negotiation Nugget**
>
> The publication Inc. identified three types of poorly done apologies: those that change the topic, those that attempt to minimize the blame, and those that wait too long to appear sincere. See, Cameron Albert-Deitch, *The 3 Types of Bad Apologies that Dominated 2017* at https://www.inc.com/cameron-albert-deitch/worst-apologies-2017.html.

3. Despite the benefits of an appropriate apology, many lawyers may be reluctant to counsel their clients to take this step, even when warranted, out of concerns for liability. For a discussion, see Jonathan R. Cohen, *Advising Clients to Apologize*, 72 S. Cal. L. Rev. 1009 (1999). Several states have enacted so-called "benevolent gesture" legislation specifically designed to address this concern. For more on this, see Jeffrey S. Helmreich, *Does 'Sorry' Incriminate? Evidence, Harm and the Protection of Apology*, Cornell J. L. Pub. Pol'y 567, 577–79 (2012); Jonathan R. Cohen, *Legislating Apology: The Pros and Cons*, 70 U. Cin. L. Rev. 819 (2002).

4. While apologies can be effective in negotiations and mediations, they have been found to be less effective in trials. See Jeffrey J. Rachlinski, Chris Guthrie & Andrew J. Wistrich, *Contrition in the Courtroom: Do Apologies Affect Adjudication*, 98 Cornell. L. Rev. 1189 (2013).

> **Digging Deeper**
>
> President Trump's persona as a hard bargainer from his days in the business world is a core part of his political image. In which world, business or politics, is it more likely for a hard-bargaining strategy to be successful? Why would that be?

4. Hard Bargaining Tactics

Those who are extreme adversarial negotiators are known as hard bargainers. They see negotiation as a game to be won and will engage in trickery and pressure tactics as a means to "win" the negotiation. These negotiators typically take advantage of information asymmetries or time constraints to exploit their negotiation counterpart's inability to confirm or refute newly asserted information. In the following excerpt, Professor Gary Goodpaster inventories several methods of adversarial tactics that hard bargainers employ. Following that piece is an excerpt by Professor James F. Westbrook explaining the approach offered in William Ury's GETTING PAST NO: NEGOTIATING WITH DIFFICULT PEOPLE (1991).

GARY GOODPASTER, A PRIMER ON COMPETITIVE BARGAINING
1996 J. Disp. Res. 325, 342–43, 349–52, 355–58, 362

The competitive negotiator adopts a risky strategy which involves the taking of firm, almost extreme positions, making few and small concessions, and withholding information that may be useful to the other party. The intention, and hoped-for effect, behind this strategy is to persuade the other party that it must make concessions if it is to get agreement. In addition to this basic strategy, competitive negotiators may also use various ploys or tactics aimed at pressuring, unsettling, unbalancing or even misleading the other party to secure an agreement with its demands.

In an important sense, the competitive negotiator plays negotiation as an information game. In this game, the object is to get as much information from the other party as possible while disclosing as little information as possible. Alternatively, a competitive negotiator sometimes provides the other party with misleading clues, bluffs, and ambiguous assertions with multiple meanings, which are not actually false, but nevertheless mislead the other party into drawing incorrect conclusions that are beneficial to the competitor.

The information the competitive negotiator seeks is the other party's bottom line. How much he will maximally give or minimally accept to make a deal. On the other hand, the competitive negotiator wants to persuade the other side about the firmness of the negotiator's own asserted bottom line. The competitive negotiator works to convince the other party that it will settle only at some point that is higher (or lower, as the case may be) than its actual and unrevealed bottom line.

* * *

Knowing these ploys and tactics gives a negotiator a clear and deeper understanding of how hard bargainers can operate throughout a negotiation on some issues or . . . when it comes time to allocate shares in whatever value the negotiators may have created. More importantly, a large part of negotiating well involves understanding how the other party is negotiating and responding appropriately. That can entail negotiating defensively, so as not to be taken, or it may involve taking the initiative and trying to change the very character of the negotiation as a process. . . . To use the game metaphor again, notwithstanding any lucky breaks, you usually can play a game well only if you understand the game you are playing.

* * *

Escalation. Escalation involves raising demands, in some way, either before or during a negotiation. Escalation before a negotiation can take the form of adding conditions before the negotiation occurs. During a negotiation, escalating demands is another way of finding the limits of what the other party is willing to give to affect an agreement. It is particularly effective when used against conciliatory or naively cooperative negotiators.

A negotiator can also escalate demands as the first move in a negotiation. Suppose, for example, two parties are meeting to discuss a proposed contract for the sale of real property for an offered price of $650,000. When the negotiation begins, the seller could state that he was sorry, but he must raise the asking price to $750,000 for a variety of reasons. The buyer, who was originally prepared to try and whittle down the $650,000 figure, now must struggle to even reach that figure. This tactic makes $650,000 look awfully good.

* * *

Other offer. To test the other party's willingness to reach an agreement or to extract concessions, a negotiator can state he has another offer or possibility and either specify what it is or deliberately leave it vague. If true, the other offer gives a baseline to judge the superiority of any pending agreement. If untrue, this is simply a tactic used to gain information or secure an advantage from the other party. Direct lies in negotiations carry considerable risks, however, particularly when the parties will have future dealings. When there is this kind of risk, those using this tactic may merely hint or imply they have another offer. This vagueness allows them to claim a misunderstanding if the other party discovers that another offer did not exist. Therefore, never accept vague assertions of the existence of other offers. . . .

> **Digging Deeper**
>
> Is there an ethical problem with using the other offer strategy when in fact there is no other offer?

False scarcity. Psychologically, people generally tend to respond to the scarcity of some item or commodity by valuing it higher. In addition, psychological reactance theory holds that when opportunities which were once open are now limited, e.g., items become scarcer or some authority imposes restrictions on conduct, people react by wanting the opportunity more than when it was more openly available. Negotiators sometimes . . . try to induce the other party into agreeing to certain positions or terms by suggesting that the opportunities are somehow quite limited.

* * *

Misleading concession pattern. In win-lose or distributive negotiations, each side uses all available information and attempts to figure out the other party's bottom line in order to extract all possible gains. Reading the concession pattern is one way to do that. In theory at least, a party will make smaller and smaller concessions as the bargaining converges on his bottom line or reservation point. Knowing that this is a common view, a negotiator can mislead the other party by planning a concession pattern which converges at a point above or below his actual bottom line. While "reading" the concession pattern, the other party may then extrapolate it to that point and mistakenly conclude that the negotiator has reached his bottom line.

* * *

Threats, anger, and aggression. The use of threats, angry displays, and aggressive tactics in a negotiation may evidence personality, frustration, or calculation. If the threat is real and the party making it can carry it out, the threat is an exercise of power and poses to the recipient the adverse consequences of a wrong choice. Negotiators, however, sometimes deliberately use such tactics simply to intimidate, disturb, and confuse the other party. As the psychological assault can unnerve and incline the victim to seek to mollify or conciliate the tantrum-thrower, negotiators using such tactics are attempting to create and to play on vulnerability in order to induce appeasement and exact concessions.

> **Note**
>
> Earlier in Chapter 3 we discussed emotion in negotiation, particularly anger.

Blaming or fault-finding. Perhaps most common in negotiations involving interpersonal issues, blaming, or assigning fault is an aggressive tactic possibly having several aims. This tactic may invoke conciliatory behavior as a result of induced guilty feelings or a sensed need to mollify. It may distract by focusing the negotiation on a substantively irrelevant, but psychologically volatile or conflictual relationship issue. "Winning" the relationship issue may result in concessions on the substantive issue. Note, however, that a person can use this tactic even in arms-length transactions where the parties do not have a psychologically invested relationship. . . .

Sudden change of mood. Sometimes, either during a single negotiation session or over the course of several sessions, a negotiator will shift radically from a reasonable, friendly tone to an angry, abusive, hostile tone or vice-versa. Such a [shift] may reflect the conscious use of psychological tactics designed to confuse the other party, place it off balance, and create vulnerability. One who is the target of another's anger often assumes, many times mistakenly, that he has somehow caused it. A natural human reaction then occurs to attempt to placate the angry person in order to smooth the situation and save the relationship. . . .

* * *

Deadline. When both sides bargain competitively but also want a deal, most concessions will likely occur toward the end of the negotiation when the deadline approaches. . . . . As a result, neither party is likely to move much until it appears absolutely necessary. Deadlines under urgency, especially externally imposed deadlines that preclude or seriously inhibit further negotiations bring the parties to the very brink of the consequences of non-agreement. Examples include the beginning of a trial, a company's need for a certain product to meet its own manufacturing deadline, or other contractual obligations. Indeed, it is as the deadline approaches that competitors are most likely to attempt to outwait the other party so that the need to settle and related time pressures will cause them to concede.

JAMES E. WESTBROOK, HOW TO NEGOTIATE WITH A JERK WITHOUT BEING ONE
1992 J. Disp. Resol. 443, 444–46

One of the most persistent questions about [the value-creation approach to negotiation] has been whether the principled negotiation approach will work if the other side takes an adversarial approach. Will the proponent of principled negotiation have to change to an adversarial approach? If she doesn't, will an impasse result? Will a negotiator using the adversarial approach take advantage of a negotiator who tries to engage in principled negotiations? [William] Ury wrote *Getting Past No* to respond to questions such as these. Of course, not everyone who takes an adversarial approach to negotiation is a jerk. I used the word jerk in my title to get your attention and because I believe it sums up a fear by many persons who are called upon to negotiate but who want to do so in a way that is consistent with their notion of appropriate conduct. Approaches such as principled negotiation appeal to these persons, but they fear that they or their client will be taken advantage of if they take such an approach. I suspect that one of their greatest concerns is that they may have to act like a jerk in order to deal effectively with a bully, a liar, or someone who is both astute and obnoxious. *Getting Past No* asserts that there is an effective alternative to relying on techniques such as deception, stonewalling, or threatening.

AN OVERVIEW OF THE BREAKTHROUGH STRATEGY

Ury recommends what he calls a "breakthrough strategy" for overcoming barriers to cooperation. He concedes that this strategy is counter-intuitive. You are called upon to do the opposite of what you might naturally do. You go around your opponent's resistance instead of meeting it head on.

The first step in the breakthrough strategy is to "go to the balcony." Instead of reacting to your opponent's tactics without thinking, you find a way to buy time. Use the time to recognize your opponent's tactics, figure out your interests, and identify your best alternative to a negotiated agreement. Much of the discussion in the chapter on going to the balcony is about the danger of making important decisions without adequate reflection and about ways of buying time for this reflection.

Second, you "step to their side" in order to create a more favorable negotiating climate. You disarm your opponent before discussing substantive issues. Ury provides a variety of ways to do this, such as asking for more information and reflecting back what you hear, acknowledging points without agreeing with them, focusing on issues on which you agree, and speaking about yourself rather than your opponent by describing the impact of the problem on yourself or your client. The chapter includes an interesting discussion about the value of an apology.

Third, reframe whatever your opponent has said as an attempt to deal with the problem. Since rejecting your opponent's position will usually reinforce it, recast what she says in a way that directs attention to satisfying interests. Ask her for advice, ask why she wants something, bring up what you think her interests are and ask her to correct you if you are wrong, ask "what if" questions, reframe your opponent's position as one possible option among many, and ask why she thinks her position is fair. Throughout, ask questions that cannot be answered by "no" by prefacing them with "how," "why," and "who." Not only do you reframe positions, but you reframe tactics. For example, if your opponent lays down a rigid deadline, reinterpret it as a target to strive for. If this cannot be done, you turn from negotiating substance to negotiating how the negotiations are to proceed. The goal here is to change the game from positional to problem-solving negotiation.

Fourth, make it easy for your opponents to say yes by "building them a golden bridge." The golden bridge chapter contains a multitude of ideas and techniques for involving your opponent in developing your proposal and for presenting it in a way that makes it easier for her to accept. Guide rather than push her toward an agreement. Consider her interests, involve her in developing your proposal, ask for and use her ideas where possible, and offer her choices. Ury suggests ways of expanding the pie by looking for low-cost, high-benefit trades and using an "if-then" formula, which deals with difficult issues by building flexible provisions into the agreement. Help her save face by showing how circumstances have changed since she adopted her position, asking for a third party recommendation, or urging reliance on a standard of fairness. Ury explains the dangers of trying to go too fast and the value of breaking the negotiation into steps.

The fifth and final step is to "make it hard to say no." This chapter contains a discussion of what to do if your opponent still resists your proposals after you have gone through the first four steps. Ury emphasizes persuasion rather than force or threats. He argues that force or threats often backfire. He suggests that you educate your opponent about the costs of not agreeing, that you warn rather than threaten, and that you demonstrate your best alternative to a negotiated agreement (BATNA). Such a demonstration shows what you will do without your actually carrying it out. Ury points out that, Power, like beauty, exists in the eyes of the beholder. If your BATNA is to have its intended educational effect of bringing your opponent back to the table, he needs to be impressed with its reality.

If you must use your BATNA, Ury recommends using as little power as possible, exhausting alternatives before escalating, and using only legitimate means. He explains the value of employing third parties where possible. As you try to persuade your opponent and as you resort to your BATNA, you need to remind her regularly of the golden bridge available to her.

POINTS FOR DISCUSSION

1.   Several hard-bargaining tactics are commonly associated with the value-claiming stages of negotiation. For lists of hard bargaining tactics other than those provided by Professor Goodpaster, see HARRY EDWARDS & JAMES J. WHITE, THE LAWYER AS NEGOTIATOR 112–21 (1977); ROBERT H. MNOOKIN, SCOTT R. PEPPET & ANDREW TULUMELLO, BEYOND WINNING: NEGOTIATING TO CREATE VALUE IN DEALS AND DISPUTES (2000); Michael Meltsner & Philip G. Schrag, *Negotiating Tactics for Legal Services Lawyers*, 7 Clearinghouse Rev. 259 (1973); D. James Greiner, Cassandra Wolos Pattanayak & Jonathan Hennessy, *The Limits of Unbundled Legal Assistance: A Randomized Study in a Massachusetts District Court and Prospects for the Future*, 126 Harv. L. Rev. 901, 919 (2013).

2.   Obviously, information asymmetries matter. If Negotiator A has access to key information and Negotiator B does not have such access, Negotiator A will be in a stronger position and may even use that strength to engage in hard bargaining on behalf of his client.

> Agents benefit from what business-school types refer to as "information asymmetry," because they are in touch with multiple teams, who are, in turn, forbidden to communicate with one another. Controlling the flow of that information—between the teams, the media, and the players—is an essential component of the Boras methodology. "In terms of negotiation, this guy is an absolute special-forces guy," a competitor said of Boras. "The prison interrogations—he's one of those." Boras is a skilled manipulator of the media, and shows the kind of patience, as deadlines approach, that derives from great self-confidence. (This spring, he cut his negotiations with the Arizona Diamondbacks over the pitcher Max Scherzer so close to the wire that the A.P. reported, at 4:42 A.M. "Diamondbacks fail to sign No. 1 pick Scherzer," only to reverse course at 5:32 A.M., with a description of a four-year deal.)

Ben McGrath, *The Extortionist*, THE NEW YORKER, Oct. 29, 2007, at 56, 60.

3.   Using information asymmetries for hard bargaining purposes can lead to impasse. Consider, for example, the following analysis of strikes:

> In the spring of 1988, television and movie writers went out on strike. The strike, which lasted for twenty-two weeks, was rhetorically bitter and economically destructive: it cost an estimated half billion dollars in lost revenues and wages and sent network

Note

In Chapter 2, we discussed studies finding that having a reputation as a distributive negotiator can negatively impact negotiation outcomes.

ratings down by nine per cent. But the walkout had only limited impact at the negotiating table: when an agreement was finally reached, it looked very much like a deal that could have been made five months earlier. The strike almost certainly cost both sides more than the sums they had been fighting over.

Twenty years later, entertainment writers are on the picket lines once again. They may do better this time, but history is against them. Walkouts may call to mind labor triumphs like the Flint sitdown strike of 1936–37, which gained union recognition for the United Automobile Workers at G.M., but most don't end that well—nor do they generally end as badly as the 1981 air-traffic controllers' strike, in which everyone got fired. Instead, strikes often end tepidly, with no major gains or rollbacks, and economists have found that, on average, strikes these days have little, if any, impact on what workers get paid. (Paradoxically, unions raise worker wages, but strikes generally don't.) Given the negative economic consequences—lost paychecks for workers and lost business for employers—the economically rational thing for both sides is usually to settle before the walkout strikes. So why don't they?

One obvious hurdle to a settlement is that neither side knows what the other side's true position is. In economists' terms, strikes happen as a result of "asymmetric information"—when one side knows more than the other about the real economics of the situation. Entertainment writers, for instance, want a share of the revenue generated from their work in new media, including programs streamed on the Internet. Producers insist that they need flexibility with regard to new technologies and that it's too early to know how much they can afford to pay for streaming programs. This may be just a bluff, or it may contain some truth—it's hard for the writers to know the difference. Going on strike is one way to find out. If a company concedes quickly, that's a sign that it was just bluffing. If it's willing to endure a long strike, that may be a sign that it meant what it said. That's why the longer a strike lasts, the less likely it is to produce a big victory for either side: you're willing to cut a deal after a long strike that you wouldn't have been willing to cut before in part because the strike has told you that the other side wasn't just bluffing.

James Surowiecki, *Striking Out*, THE NEW YORKER, Nov. 19, 2007, 42.

4. Not all strike situations have limited impacts on the parties' respective interests. For example, in 2012, the Chicago Teacher's Union went on strike in reaction to then Chicago Mayor Rahm Emanuel's demand for longer school days without extra teacher compensation. In return, Mayor Emanuel widely known as a political "tough guy" went to court asking for an injunction to stop the strike. After eight-days on strike and under the threat of an injunction, the Chicago Teacher's

Union reached an agreement with the Mayor, who called it an "honest compromise." The mayor got longer school days he was seeking, and the union members received extra compensation for their longer hours of work. Monica Davey, *Teachers End Chicago Strike on Second Try*, The NY Times, September 18, 2012. Who was trying to assert power here—the union or the mayor? Why do you think the parties were unable to reach an agreement before the mayor filed a lawsuit? Are hard-bargaining tactics assertions of power or rights, or are they something else? When might these assertions be helpful and when might they be harmful?

5.   Some of the risks associated with a negotiation approach that emphasizes claiming value include alienating others, inefficient and unsustainable agreements, and reaching impasse when a deal was there for the making. These risks are dramatically amplified with hard bargaining. William Ury's GETTING PAST NO: NEGOTIATING WITH DIFFICULT PEOPLE (1991) included a simple strategy for addressing hard bargainers—reframe their tactics as a means to engage in the value creating approach to negotiation. Doing so had been suggested in earlier works, but GETTING PAST NO made its mark by providing a clear method of how to do so.

6.   As you read Professor Westbrook's description of Mr. Ury's method, did you buy in or were you skeptical? Why? Are there times when this approach would be more or less effective?

7.   What should a lawyer who favors the value-creation approach to negotiation do if his client asks him to use more strong-armed tactics during the negotiation? What if the client asks him to back off from using strong-armed tactics?

D. COMMITMENT

The final stage of the negotiation process is where the parties either commit to each other, in the form of a written agreement, or commit to walk away from the potential agreement and to their respective BATNAs. Reaching a deal is not the only important outcome of a negotiation. And whether the negotiation ends in a deal is not the be-all and end-all. How the negotiation ends is important as well. For example, if a negotiation ends in impasse are reputational concerns or ongoing relationships important? If so, is there a way to exit graciously? Or, should a message be sent to influence another negotiator's future conduct? These are important questions for consideration.

Nonetheless, we focus here on negotiations moving toward agreement. In the following excerpt, Professor Charles B. Craver suggests that negotiators look to enhance the value of the deal for both sides once they sense that a deal is looming.

CHARLES B. CRAVER, SKILLS AND VALUES: LEGAL NEGOTIATING
46–47 (2d ed. 2012)

By the conclusion of the [Offer and Concession] Stage, *both sides* have become psychologically committed to a joint resolution. Neither wants their prior bargaining efforts to culminate in failure. Less proficient negotiators focus almost entirely on their own side's desire for an agreement, completely disregarding the settlement pressure on their opponents. [At this time], *both sides* want an agreement. It is thus appropriate for both parties to expect joint movement toward final terms. Negotiators should be careful not to make unreciprocated concessions, and to avoid excessive position changes.

* * *

Once a tentative accord has been reached through the distributive process, the negotiators should contemplate alternative trade-offs that might concurrently enhance the interests of both parties. The bargainers may be mentally, and even physically, exhausted from their prior discussions, but they should at least briefly explore alternative formulations that may prove to be mutually advantageous. During [earlier stages], the parties often over- or under-state the actual value of different items for strategic reasons. During [the offer and concession stage], they tend to be cautious and opportunistic. Both sides are likely to employ power bargaining tactics designed to achieve results favorable to their own circumstances. Because of the tension created by these distributive techniques, * * * superior arrangements are rarely attained by this point in the negotiation process. The participants are likely to have only achieved "acceptable" terms. If they conclude their interaction at this point, they may leave a substantial amount of untapped joint satisfaction on the bargaining table.

POINTS FOR DISCUSSION

1. Martin E. Latz describes commitment as a two-stage process—the initial close and the final close. The initial close is when offers and concessions come in quick succession, and the final close is when the deal is documented. In the initial close, he advises that appearing patient is crucial, confirming knowledge of your counterpart's interests (especially those that might prevent an agreement), and creating an appropriate sense of urgency to complete the negotiation. GAIN THE EDGE: NEGOTIATING TO GET WHAT YOU WANT 204 (2004). The final close is where drafting comes in. He suggests quickly confirming all oral commitments in

writing and getting a draft of a proposed deal to your counterpart promptly. *Id.* at 205.

2.   While contract drafting is not a focus in this book, drafting the contract is a critical part of the negotiation process. Not only does the drafting memorialize the deal going forward, the drafting process may also bring to the fore issues yet to be contemplated and result in additional terms being negotiated. Professor Tina L. Stark provides several important suggestions to keep in mind when drafting a contract: accurately memorializing the deal, being clear and unambiguous, resolving problems pragmatically, and being specific enough that the parties know their rights and obligations while also flexible enough to cope with changed circumstances. Professor Stark describes the process of determining the contract concepts that best reflect the terms of the deal as a "translation skill." What do you think she means by that? Tina L. Stark, DRAFTING CONTRACTS: HOW AND WHY LAWYERS DO WHAT THEY DO 4, 10 (2007).

Negotiation Nugget

Writing a clear and unambiguous agreement is more difficult than one would anticipate. One thing to keep in mind is the audience. Will someone who was not at the negotiation table understand what the obligations are for each party? To help in this regard use simple subject-verb-object sentences and bullet points to make contracts easier to read.

3.   In most cases, some continued bargaining during the final closing stage is not problematic. In certain circumstances, however, it can be, particularly when negotiators engage in the negotiation tactic known as nibbling. Nibbling occurs once everyone has agreed that they have a deal on a specific set of terms, but one of the negotiators asks for a little bit of movement on one of the terms in hopes that the counterpart will concede in order to save the deal. This tactic preys on the psychological commitment to the deal that Professor Craver described above.

Digging Deeper

Is the "nibbling" technique described by Craver ethical? If so why, and if not why not?

4.   Once the deal is drafted, the clients still must approve it. Sometimes this is easy, but at other times, getting approval can be more difficult. In most cases clients are involved in the drafting process, seeing drafts of the contract language and approving it as the drafting is going on. This process is more difficult when one party is a governmental entity or other organization that requires board approval before a deal can be officially accepted. Whether one is negotiating with a public or private

entity, it is best to know at the outset who will have the authority to approve a final deal.

CHAPTER 4

PRINCIPALS AND AGENTS

Most people conduct the vast majority of their negotiations without help from lawyers or other agents. See, e.g., ROBERT C. ELLICKSON, ORDER WITHOUT LAW: HOW NEIGHBORS SETTLE DISPUTES (1991). Even in disputes involving potentially legally actionable claims, people seldom retain lawyers to represent them. One famous study is illustrative. Richard Miller and Austin Sarat contacted individuals by telephone to inquire about potentially legally remediable injuries that members of their households had suffered. Out of every 1,000 such instances, individuals hired lawyers on only 100 occasions. See Richard E. Miller & Austin Sarat, *Grievances, Claims, and Disputes: Assessing the Adversary Culture*, 15 Law & Soc'y Rev. 525, 534–46 (1980–81).

Despite the relative infrequency with which individuals hire lawyers, lawyers nonetheless represent many clients in transactional negotiations and dispute settlements. Adding clients to the equation introduces another variable into the negotiation calculus. The following excerpt discusses the benefits of having an agent negotiate on behalf of a principal and the problems arising from the principal-agent relationship that lawyers regularly experience.

ROBERT H. MNOOKIN, SCOTT R. PEPPET, ANDRE S. TULUMELLO, BEYOND WINNING: NEGOTIATING TO CREATE VALUE IN DEALS AND DISPUTES
70–71, 74–76 (2000)

When a principal hires an agent to act on his behalf in negotiations across the table with another party, he may expect—naively—that the agent will be motivated to serve the principal's interests. This is how principal-agent relations would work ideally. But in the real world, agents always have interests of their own. As a result, the principal-agent relationship is rife with potential conflicts that demand skillful management behind the table.

For example, a client and his lawyer may need to negotiate how the lawyer will be paid; how the other side will be approached; what information will be sought from or disclosed to the other side; at what point to accept the other side's offer, and so on. If these issues are left unacknowledged and unaddressed, they can adversely affect the negotiation across the table. For all of these reasons, effective negotiation requires a good understanding of the benefits and risks of the agency relationships and how it can best be managed.

Agency Benefits

Why are agency relationships so pervasive in negotiation? Because an agent can provide significant benefits to her principal. These benefits derive from four sources:

- Knowledge: An agent may have specialized knowledge—that the principal lacks—about market conditions, formal or informal norms, or relevant risks and opportunities. . . .

- Resources: An agent, by reason of his reputation and relationships, may be able to provide access and opportunities that would otherwise be unavailable. . . .

- Skills: An agent may be a better negotiator than the principal, whether owing to experience, training, or natural ability. . . .

- Strategic Advantages: An agent may be able to use negotiation tactics on behalf of the principal in a way that insulates the principal from their full impact. The principal can remain the "good cop" while the agent plays the bad cop. . . .

In many cases, the agent will be able to do things the principal could never do on his own, and the possibility for both the principal and agent to benefit from the trade is clear.

* * *

The Problem: Agency Costs

Hiring an agent is not a simple matter. . . . [The principal-agent relationship] can create value. At the same time, however, because the agent's interests may not align with those of the principal, a number of unique and intensely stubborn problems can arise. . . . Here, we introduce some of the central issues.

The Sources of the Tension

Agency costs are not limited to the amount of money that a principal pays an agent as compensation for doing the job. They also include the money and time the principal spends trying to ensure that the agent does not exploit him but instead serves his interests as well. To understand why agency costs exist, consider that principals and agents may differ in three general ways: preferences, incentives, [and] information.

Different Preferences

First, the preferences, or interests, of an agent are rarely identical to those of the principal. [In a sale of a house, a real estate agent's] primary interest is in her own earnings. . . . [The seller's] primary economic interest is in the net sales price for his house. [The realtor] also has a strong interest in her reputation and in securing future clients. She has an interest in maintaining good relationships with other agents, banks, home inspectors, and insurance agencies. [She] is a repeat player in this game while [the seller], particularly if he is leaving the community, is a one-shot player who might be more than willing to sacrifice [the agent's] reputation to get a better deal for himself. Conversely, [the agent] may be reluctant to bargain hard for certain advantages. . . . because of her desire to maintain a congenial relationship with the buyer's agent, who may be a source of future client referrals.

Different Incentives

Agency problems may also arise because the *incentives* of the principal and agent are imperfectly aligned. The culprit is typically the agent's fee structure, which may create perverse incentives for the agent to act contrary to the principal's interest. . . .

For example, [the seller] wants an arrangement that maximizes his expected net sale proceeds after her fee. [The realtor], on the other hand, wants a fee structure that yields her the highest expected return *for her time spent.* If they agree to a percentage fee, [the realtor] may prefer a quick and easy sale at a lower price to a difficult sale at a higher price because with the former she will get more return for hours spent working. . . .

Different Information

The information available to the principal and agent may differ. We are speaking here of kinds of information that either side may have an incentive to keep to itself. [The realtor] may know that market conditions are improving, for example, but she may be reluctant to share with [the seller] for fear of inflating his expectations. Similarly, it may be difficult to know how much effort an agent is actually putting in on the principal's behalf. Because the principal cannot readily discover this information, the agent might shirk her responsibilities and earn pay without expending effort.

POINTS FOR DISCUSSION

1.   Many lawyers find negotiations with their clients to be among their most difficult negotiations. Why would that be?

2.   How do lawyers and clients manage their differences with respect to incentives? In BEYOND WINNING, Mnookin, Peppet, and Tulumello identify several different fee structures to do this: contingency fee, fixed fee, hourly fee, mixed fee, and salary. What are the pros and cons of each with respect to how attorneys negotiate on behalf of their clients?

3.   Understanding what the client wants and why the client wants it can be difficult. To facilitate conversation with the client and to help in negotiation preparation, Professor Charles B. Craver suggests dividing client goals into categories.

> **Negotiation Nugget**
>
> Many people in the corporate world see their company's legal department as the place where good ideas and deals go to die. Thus, they may view in-house counsel as more of an adversary than their negotiation counterparts. In-house counsel are wise to develop collaborative relationships with their clientele to develop trust that can be drawn upon when necessary.

> Most legal representatives formally or informally divide client goals into three categories: (1) essential, (2) important, and (3) desirable. Essential items include terms clients must obtain if agreements are to be successfully achieved. Important goals concern things clients really want to acquire, but which they would be willing to exchange for essential or other important items. Desirable needs involve items of secondary value which clients would be pleased to obtain, but which they would exchange for "essential" or "important" terms.

CHARLES B. CRAVER, SKILLS & VALUES: LEGAL NEGOTIATING 20 (2d ed. 2012). Is a more adversarial approach to negotiation implied in this advice? If so, how might a negotiator with a value-creating approach reframe this suggestion?

4.   In BEYOND WINNING, Mnookin, Peppet, and Tulumello describe the negotiation between a principal and agent as the "behind the table negotiation" as compared to the "across the table" negotiation with their negotiation counterpart. Should lawyers approach the behind the table negotiation differently than any other negotiation? Which approach to negotiation best serves the lawyer-client relationship? Presuming that lawyers should memorialize solutions to principal-agent problems in their engagement letters and representation contracts, what form should these terms take?

5.   When discussing client preferences with respect to negotiation goals and aspirations, outcomes, and strategy, how should a lawyer discuss those differences with the client? What if the lawyer finds the client's expectations regarding outcome to be utterly unreasonable? Mnookin, Peppet, and Tulumello suggest the following:

> Labeling your client as unreasonable is not the best way to establish a process for talking about legal risk. Where do these "unreasonable" expectations come from? Maybe your client is legally sophisticated and simply reasons to a different conclusion from the same legal precedents you've read. Maybe your client has factual information about the case that you don't. Maybe the client is simply more open to running risks that you would not. You should be open to learning that your client might be operating on different basic premises than you are.
>
> * * *
>
> Sometimes clients set their expectations in terms of what they want, rather than in terms of legal opportunities and risks. A client might say "I'll only pay $1,200 a month child support and not a penny more." If you think this is unrealistic, you need to explain why.
>
> Don't ease in. If you beat around the bush, hedge, or qualify, your client may become frustrated, apprehensive, or angry. It's not hard to tell when someone is being evasive. It's better to put the bad news up front and empathize as your client reacts. . . . If the client remains unpersuaded, give him some time. Sometimes a client needs time to let go of his initial aspirations, even in the face of solid legal advice. Or you may need to raise it again. If the client persists, and you've explained your reasons well, you might follow the client's direction even though you disagree. Alternatively, if the stakes are high enough, the client may find it helpful to get a second opinion. Perhaps there's someone else in the firm who could offer an assessment. Or there may be a respected outsider who could be consulted.

ROBERT H. MNOOKIN, SCOTT R. PEPPET & ANDREW S. TULUMELLO, BEYOND WINNING: NEGOTIATING TO CREATE VALUE IN DEALS AND DISPUTES 199 (2000).

CHAPTER 5

ETHICAL AND LEGAL LIMITATIONS

This chapter surveys the boundaries of acceptable negotiation conduct. Specifically, Subsection A explores the restraints the ethical rules for lawyers in the United States impose upon lawyer-negotiators. In Subsection B, we explore the legal limitations imposed on all negotiators by the law.

> **Digging Deeper**
>
> Are there other ethical standards such as general morality or fairness that may apply in the bargaining situation?

A. ATTORNEY NEGOTIATION ETHICS

Negotiators frequently find themselves confronted with difficult questions they would rather not answer. While most aspire to being truthful, being too truthful can be harmful to one's leverage and even lead to exploitation. Evasion may be more palatable than lying, but it can signal less than full disclosure. And deception, no matter how it is described, may help negotiators reach their short-term goals, but might have serious long-term consequences. To complicate matters further, lawyers must follow the ethical rules regulating the legal profession. This complex scenario has the potential to create a difficult balancing act when the ethical rules' obligations appear to be in tension with the obligations the lawyer faces as an advocate for her client.

> **Negotiation Nugget**
>
> California is the only state that has not based its legal ethics rules on the ABA Model Rules. But Californians would still be wise to know these rules.

All but one state have patterned their professional responsibility rules after the ABA's Model Rules of Professional Conduct. The preamble to the Model Rules provides that a lawyer is "a member of the legal profession," "a representative of clients, an officer of the legal system and a public citizen having special responsibility for the quality of justice," and that "[a]s negotiator, a lawyer seeks a result advantageous to the client but consistent with requirements of honest dealings with others." MODEL RULES OF PROF'L CONDUCT Preamble (2013).

In the following two excerpts note how the rules of professional conduct address improper attorney negotiation conduct. The first excerpt, by Professor James J. White, discusses the difficulties of requiring attorneys to be fair in their negotiations. The second, by Professors Art Hinshaw and Jess K. Alberts, discusses how the Model Rules of Professional Conduct approach dissembling in negotiation.

JAMES J. WHITE, MACHIAVELLI AND THE BAR: ETHICAL LIMITATIONS ON LYING IN NEGOTIATION
1980 Am. B. Found. Res. J. 926, 927–29, 931–35

[In this excerpt, Professor White is commenting on a proposed ethical rule that would have required, in part, that lawyers "be fair in dealing with others." This rule was not adopted into the Model Rules of Professional Conduct.]

On the one hand the negotiator must be fair and truthful; on the other he must mislead his opponent. Like the poker player, a negotiator hopes that his opponent will overestimate the value of his hand. Like the poker player, in a variety of ways he must facilitate his opponent's inaccurate assessment. The critical difference between those who are successful negotiators and those who are not lies in this capacity both to mislead and not to be misled.

Some experienced negotiators will deny the accuracy of this assertion, but they will be wrong. I submit that a careful examination of the behavior of even the most forthright, honest, and trustworthy negotiators will show them actively engaged in misleading their opponents about their true positions. That is true of both the plaintiff and the defendant in a lawsuit. It is true of both labor and management in a collective bargaining agreement. It is true as well of both the buyer and the seller in a wide variety of sales transactions. To conceal one's true position, to mislead an opponent about one's true settling point, is the essence of negotiation.

Of course there are limits on acceptable deceptive behavior in negotiation, but there is the paradox. How can one be "fair" but also mislead? Can we ask the negotiator to mislead, but fairly, like the soldier who must kill, but humanely?

TRUTHTELLING IN GENERAL

The obligation to behave truthfully in negotiation is embodied in the requirement of Rule 4.2(a) that directs the lawyer to "be fair in dealing with other participants."

* * *

The comment on fairness under Rule 4.2 makes explicit what is implicit in the rule itself by the following sentence: "Fairness in negotiation implies that representations by or on behalf of one party to the other party be truthful." Standing alone that statement is too broad. Even the Comments contemplate activities such as puffing which, in the broadest sense, are untruthful. It seems quite unlikely that the drafters intend or can realistically hope to outlaw a variety of other nontruthful behavior in negotiations.

* * *

FIVE CASES

[I]t is probably important to give more than the simple disclaimer about the impossibility of defining the appropriate limits of puffing that the drafters have given in the current Comments. To test these limits, consider five cases. Easiest is the question that arises when one misrepresents his true opinion about the meaning of a case or a statute. Presumably such a misrepresentation is accepted lawyer behavior both in and out of court and is not intended to be precluded by the requirement that the lawyer be "truthful." In writing his briefs, arguing his case, and attempting to persuade the opposing party in negotiation, it is the lawyer's right and probably his responsibility to argue for plausible interpretations of cases and statutes which favor his client's interest, even in circumstances where privately he has advised his client that those are not his true interpretations of the cases and statutes.

A second form of distortion that the Comments plainly envision as permissible is distortion concerning the value of one's case or of the other subject matter involved in the negotiation. Thus the Comments make explicit reference to "puffery." Presumably they are attempting to draw the same line that one draws in commercial law between express warranties and "mere puffing" under section 2–313 of the Uniform Commercial Code. While this line is not easy to draw, it generally means that the seller of a product has the right to make general statements concerning the value of his product without having the law treat those statements as warranties and without having liability if they turn out to be inaccurate estimates of the value. As the statements descend toward greater and greater particularity, as the ignorance of the person receiving the statements increases, the courts are likely to find them to be not puffing but express warranties. By the same token a lawyer could make assertions about his case or about the subject matter of his negotiation in general terms, and if those proved to be inaccurate, they would not be a violation of the ethical standards. Presumably such statements are not violations of the ethical standards even when they conflict with the lawyer's dispassionate analysis of the value of his case.

A third case is related to puffing but different from it. This is the use of the so-called false demand. It is a standard negotiating technique in collective bargaining negotiation and in some other multiple-issue negotiations for one side to include a series of demands about which it cares little or not at all. The purpose of including these demands is to increase one's supply of negotiating currency. One hopes to convince the other party that one or more of these false demands is important and thus successfully to trade it for some significant concession. The assertion of and argument for a false demand involves the same kind of distortion that is involved in puffing or in arguing the merits of cases or statutes that are not really controlling. The proponent of a false demand implicitly or explicitly states his interest in the demand and his estimation of it. Such behavior is untruthful in the broadest sense; yet at least in collective bargaining negotiation its use is a standard part of the process and is not thought to be inappropriate by any experienced bargainer.

Two final examples may be more troublesome. The first involves the response of a lawyer to a question from the other side. Assume that the defendant has instructed his lawyer to accept any settlement offer under $100,000. Having received that instruction, how does the defendant's lawyer respond to the plaintiff's question, "I think $90,000 will settle this case. Will your client give $90,000?" Do you see the dilemma that question poses for the defense lawyer? It calls for information that would not have to be disclosed. A truthful answer to it concludes the negotiation and dashes any possibility of negotiating a lower settlement even in circumstances in which the plaintiff might be willing to accept half of $90,000. Even a moment's hesitation in response to the question may be a nonverbal communication to a clever plaintiff's lawyer that the defendant has given such authority. Yet a negative response is a lie.

It is no answer that a clever lawyer will answer all such questions about authority by refusing to answer them, nor is it an answer that some lawyers will be clever enough to tell their clients not to grant them authority to accept a given sum until the final stages in negotiation. Most of us are not that careful or that clever. Few will routinely refuse to answer such questions in cases in which the client has granted a much lower limit than that discussed by the other party, for in that case an honest answer about the absence of authority is a quick and effective method of changing the opponent's settling point, and it is one that few of us will forego when our authority is far below that requested by the other party. Thus despite the fact that a clever negotiator can avoid having to lie or to reveal his settling point, many lawyers, perhaps most, will sometime be forced by such a question either to lie or to reveal that they have been granted such authority by saying so or by their silence in response to a direct question. Is it fair to lie in such a case?

> **Negotiation Nugget**
>
> One should not disclose to a counterpart the authority a client has given with respect to a negotiation. Instead, the lawyer should restate the previous offer/demand by saying something like "my client is asking for . . .," redirect the conversation, ignore the question, or politely say something like "you know I can't disclose that."

Before one examines the possible justifications for a lie in that circumstance, consider a final example recently suggested to me by a lawyer in practice. There the lawyer represented three persons who had been charged with shoplifting. Having satisfied himself that there was no significant conflict of interest, the defense lawyer told the prosecutor that two of the three would plead guilty only if the case was dismissed against the third. Previously those two had told the defense counsel that they would plead guilty irrespective of what the third did, and the third had said that he wished to go to trial unless the charges were dropped. Thus the defense lawyer lied to the prosecutor by stating that the two would plead only if the third were allowed to go free. Can the lie be justified in this case?

How does one distinguish the cases where truthfulness is not required and those where it is required? Why do the first three cases seem easy? I suggest they are easy cases because the rules of the game are explicit and well developed in those areas. Everyone expects a lawyer to distort the value of his own case, of his own facts and arguments, and to deprecate those of his opponent. No one is surprised by that, and the system accepts and expects that behavior. To a lesser extent the same is true of the false demand procedure in labor-management negotiations where the ploy is sufficiently widely used to be explicitly identified in the literature. A layman might say that this behavior falls within the ambit of "exaggeration," a form of behavior that while not necessarily respected is not regarded as morally reprehensible in our society.

The last two cases are more difficult. In one the lawyer lies about his authority; in the other he lies about the intention of his clients. It would be more difficult to justify the lies in those cases by arguing that the rules of the game explicitly permit that sort of behavior. Some might say that the rules of the game provide for such distortion, but I suspect that many lawyers would say that such lies are out of bounds and are not part of the rules of the game. Can the lie about authority be justified on the ground that the question itself was improper? Put another way, if I have a right to keep certain information to myself, and if any behavior but a lie will reveal that information to the other side, am I justified in lying? I think not. Particularly in the case in which there are other avenues open to the respondent, should we not ask him to take those avenues? That is, the careful negotiator here can turn aside all such questions and by doing so avoid any inference from his failure to answer such questions.

What makes the last case a close one? Conceivably it is the idea that one accused by the state is entitled to greater leeway in making his case. Possibly one can argue that there is no injury to the state when such a person, particularly an innocent person, goes free. Is it conceivable that the act can be justified on the ground that it is part of the game in this context, that prosecutors as well as defense lawyers routinely misstate what they, their witnesses, and their clients can and will do? None of these arguments seems persuasive. Justice is not served by freeing a guilty person. The system does not necessarily achieve better results by trading two guilty pleas for a dismissal. Perhaps its justification has its roots in the same idea that formerly held that a misrepresentation of one's state of mind was not actionable for it was not a misrepresentation of fact.

In a sense rules governing these cases may simply arise from a recognition by the law of its limited power to shape human behavior. By tolerating exaggeration and puffing in the sales transaction, by refusing to make misstatement of one's intention actionable, the law may simply have recognized the bounds of its control over human behavior. Having said that, one is still left with the question, Are the lies permissible in the last two cases?

My general conclusion is that they are not, but I am not nearly as comfortable with that conclusion as I am with the conclusion about the first three cases.

Taken together, the five foregoing cases show me that we do not and cannot intend that a negotiator be "truthful" in the broadest sense of that term. At the minimum we allow him some deviation from truthfulness in asserting his true opinion about cases, statutes, or the value of the subject of the negotiation in other respects. In addition some of us are likely to allow him to lie in response to certain questions that are regarded as out of bounds, and possibly to lie in circumstances where his interest is great and the injury seems small. It would be unfortunate, therefore, for the rule that requires "fairness" to be interpreted to require that a negotiator be truthful in every respect and in all of his dealings. It should be read to allow at least those kinds of untruthfulness that are implicitly and explicitly recognized as acceptable in his forum, a forum defined both by the subject matter and by the participants.

ART HINSHAW & JESS K. ALBERTS, DOING THE RIGHT THING: AN EMPIRICAL STUDY OF ATTORNEY NEGOTIATION ETHICS
16 Harv. Neg. L. Rev. 95, 102–106 (2011)

The Model Rules' drafters assumed that lawyers would act in the role of a partisan representative on behalf of their clients against the interests of third parties. To keep their partisan ethos from crossing into unlawful territory, Rule 4.1, "Truthfulness in Statements to Others," imposes limits on the deception lawyers can use. Rule 4.1 provides:

In the course of representing a client, a lawyer shall not knowingly:

(a) Make a false statement of material fact or law to a third person; or

(b) Fail to disclose a material fact to a third person when disclosure is necessary to avoid assisting a criminal or fraudulent act by a client, unless disclosure is prohibited by Rule 1.6.

A simple proposition lies at the Rule's core: lawyers may act as partisans for their clients, but they must draw the line at lying. Lying includes overt lies, active misrepresentations, as well as misrepresentations by omission. Underlying the Rule is one of the foundational propositions in the Model Rules—that attorneys should not participate in a client's criminal or fraudulent conduct. Although Rule 4.1's text appears straightforward, the Rule's application is not.

a.   Rule 4.1(a)

The first issue arises because Rule 4.1(a)'s prohibition applies only to "material" facts or law. However, the Model Rules fail to define the term "material," instead explaining that what constitutes a material fact "depends on the circumstances." Generally, a statement of fact is considered material if it is significant or essential to the negotiation, but Comment 2 explains:

> Under generally accepted conventions in negotiation, certain types of statements ordinarily are not taken as statements of material fact.

It then provides examples of statements that ordinarily fall into this immaterial fact category, including estimates of price or value and a party's intentions as to an acceptable settlement of a claim, arguably the two most material matters during bargaining interactions. The Comment's phrasing also suggests that this is not an exclusive list, and many authorities have surmised that other types of statements must not be material facts because they fall into the "generally accepted negotiation conventions" category. However, it is unclear what those other statements might be.

Defining the Rule's determinative principle by explaining what it is not leads to difficulties in interpretation. When grappling with this problem, only one court has defined the term "material fact" using verbiage other than what appears in the Rule's Comments, and it did so in positive terms:

> A fact is material to a negotiation if it reasonably may be viewed as important to a fair understanding of what is being given up and, in return, gained by the [deal].[32]

This definition underscores the breadth of the term "material fact," which explains why Comment 2 narrows it. The two keys to determining whether a fact is material in the context of Rule 4.1 are: (a) whether the fact has a reasonable effect on one party's understanding of what is being negotiated, and (b) whether the statement is an estimate of price or value on the subject of a transaction or a party's intentions as to an acceptable settlement of a claim.

Rule 4.1(a) forbids false statements of material law as well as false statements of material fact. The Rule's Comments do not address what constitutes "material law," leaving lawyers with a dictionary definition: law that is either significant or essential to the negotiation. Rule 4.1's prohibition

---

[32] *Ausherman v. Bank of Am. Corp.*, 212 F. Supp. 2d 435, 449 (D. Md. 2002), *aff'd* 352 F.3d 896 (4th Cir. 2003).

regarding material law is most often germane when a statement is addressed to a non-lawyer, but it applies to opposing counsel and judges as well.

Thus, when speaking to others about material issues, Rule 4.1(a) simply requires lawyers to speak the truth as they understand it without engaging in any misrepresentations. However, a lawyer is *not* prohibited from making deliberate misrepresentations about non-material facts or law to anyone.

b. Rule 4.1(b)

Generally, lawyers have no duty voluntarily to inform an opposing party of relevant facts when negotiating. Under the auspices of Rule 4.1(b), however, a duty to disclose material facts or law arises only if doing so avoids assisting in a client's criminal conduct or fraud. In other words, the lawyer's silence may cause the lawyer to be complicit in a fraudulent misrepresentation by omission. In instances where nondisclosure constitutes a fraudulent misrepresentation, such as when the lawyer finds that her work has unwittingly been used to further an ongoing fraud, the lawyer has a duty to correct the misapprehension.

Yet the Rule provides that disclosure is proper only if it does not violate the duty of maintaining client confidences stated in Rule 1.6. This would appear to vitiate the duty of disclosure, allowing lawyers to participate in a client's crime or fraud. However, reading Rule 4.1(b) with Rule 1.6 and with the values behind the Model Rules negates such a conclusion. Rule 1.6 contains several discretionary exceptions permitting disclosure with respect to criminal or fraudulent conduct in order to prevent, mitigate, or rectify injuries due to conduct for which the lawyer's services have been unwittingly used.[42] But these permissive reporting requirements become mandatory "when disclosure is necessary to avoid assisting a criminal or fraudulent act by a client." Similarly, the general requirements of Rule 1.6 have always been subject to Rule 1.2(d)'s prohibition against knowingly participating in a client's criminal or fraudulent conduct. Thus, the reference to client confidential information in Rule 4.1(b) does not modify the duty to disclose material facts when doing so would avoid assisting the client's criminal conduct or fraud.

If a client asks an attorney to engage in criminal or fraudulent acts, the attorney and client should first discuss the consequences of the client's request and, if the client refuses to reconsider the action, the lawyer should withdraw from the representation. If the lawyer withdraws, she may still be

---

[42] Model Rules of Prof'l Conduct r. 1.6(b)(2), (3) (Am. Bar Assn. 1983).

required to disaffirm any fraudulent statement with which she might be deemed to be associated by reason of the prior representation.

Rule 4.1's regulation on attorney negotiation behavior is modest notwithstanding its prohibition of fraudulent conduct and assisting in a client's fraudulent conduct. The Rule allows attorneys to be deceitful about opinions and non-material facts and law, which allows for puffing and bluffing. Furthermore, technical violations of Rule 4.1 where no one is harmed are unlikely to be the subject of disciplinary proceedings or court sanctions. In practice, Rule 4.1 does little other than proscribe fraudulent misrepresentations in negotiation.

POINTS FOR DISCUSSION

1.   Is Professor White correct that a negotiator "must be fair and truthful" on the one hand but that he "must mislead his opponent" on the other? In each of the five cases Professor White discusses, do you agree with his conclusions about whether it is permissible to mislead your counterpart?

2.   In their excerpted article, Professors Hinshaw and Alberts presented the results of a study in which they gave lawyers an ethical dilemma involving the continuation of a client's misrepresentation, the truth of which, if known, would have severely compromised what would otherwise have been a substantial claim. Here's what they found:

> The aggregated results of the survey, which report the findings from 734 respondents from the Phoenix, Arizona and St. Louis, Missouri metropolitan areas, found that in response to the client's initial request to refrain from [providing the true information], 62 percent of the respondents said that they would not agree to such a request, while 19 percent said they would agree to the client's request. The remaining 19 percent of the respondents indicated they were not sure how they would respond if placed in this situation. The responses to the client's second request—to disclose [the true information] only if directly asked [about it]—revealed similar results. Sixty-four percent of these respondents (592 respondents) indicated they would refuse the request, 13 percent indicated that they would agree, and 23 percent replied that they were not sure what they would do.
>
>   * * *
>
> When combining the results of the client's two requests, we found that 30 percent of the respondents agreed to engage in the fraudulent settlement negotiation scheme in violation of Rule 4.1, 50 percent of the

respondents refused both client requests, thereby following the proper course of action, and the remaining 20 percent responded that they were unsure how to respond to one or both requests. The study also revealed that potential reasons for this problem include considerable confusion among some attorneys regarding the elements of Rule 4.1. That is, just more than a quarter of the respondents failed to recognize that refraining from disclosing the [true information] constituted a misrepresentation, and many were unable to properly identify various material facts in the hypothetical negotiation. The study also revealed that many attorneys believe that confidentiality concerns, such as client confidentiality and the attorney-client privilege, trump the Model Rule's dictates to refrain from assisting clients in fraudulent conduct.

Art Hinshaw & Jess K. Alberts, *Gender and Attorney Negotiation Ethics*, 39 Wash. U. J.L. & Pol'y 145, 155–157 (2012).

3.   A negotiator might mislead a counterpart by making untrue statements (*lying by commission*), by failing to disclose pertinent information (*lying by omission*), or by making true statements in order to create a false impression (*paltering*). As an empirical matter, lying by commission tends to be perceived as more objectionable than lying by omission, and people tend to be more willing to lie by omission than by commission. Research has also found that paltering is more likely than lying by commission and is seen by the negotiator making the statement as less unethical than lying by commission. But paltering is viewed by negotiation counterparts as equally as unethical as lying by commission and results in damage to the negotiator's reputation if the deception is discovered. Todd Rogers, Richard Zeckhauser, Francesca Gino, Michael I. Norton, & Maurice E. Schweitzer, *Artful Paltering: The Risks and Rewards of Using Truthful Statements to Mislead Others*, 112 J. Personality & Soc. Psychol. 456 (2017).

4.   If price or value are "ordinarily not taken as statements of fact," is a lawyer's authority from a client a material fact or is it viewed like the price or value of an item? An ABA ethics opinion on the issue concludes that in certain circumstances it can be a material fact. Specifically, Opinion 06–439 states:

> [C]are must be taken by the lawyer to ensure that communications regarding the client's position, which otherwise would not be considered statements "of fact," are not conveyed in language that converts them, even inadvertently, into false factual representations. . . . [I]t would not be permissible for [a] lawyer to state that [a client's] Board of Directors has formally disapproved any settlement in excess of $50, when authority had in fact been granted to settle for a higher sum.

ABA Comm'n on Ethics & Prof'l Responsibility, Formal Op. 06–439 (2006).

In the context of Rule 4.1, price and value are treated as if they are questions of opinion—subjective issues influenced by a host of factors. But once a statement becomes verifiable and objective, like the Board of Director's vote, it is objectively true or false and no longer a matter of opinion. Do you think it is a good idea for a lawyer to disclose the negotiation authority a client has given him? If so, how should a lawyer best do that? Are there any other rules that impact whether a lawyer should disclose that information?

Digging Deeper

The Model Rules of Professional Responsibility discuss ethics as more of a limbo type process—how low can you go and still be ok? Should ethical standards be prohibitions or more aspirational in character, especially with regard to truthfulness?

5. Two other Model Rules also directly impact the negotiation process. The first, Rule 3.3 "Candor to the Tribunal," states that attorneys shall not knowingly "make false statements of fact or law" to a tribunal, which includes judges, arbitrators, and other hearing panels. The rule applies to any statement of fact, not just statements of material fact. Thus, lawyers need to be on their guard not to violate this rule when in judicial settlement conferences, particularly when describing the various components of offers and counteroffers. See *In re Fee*, 898 P.2d 975 (Ariz. 1995) (finding a violation of Rule 3.3 when lawyers failed to correct a settlement conference judge's misunderstanding of their fee agreement with their client).

The second rule in this category is Rule 8.4, simply titled "Misconduct," which applies in all lawyering contexts. As it applies to negotiation, Rule 8.4(c) specifically defines "dishonesty, fraud, deceit, or misrepresentation" as misconduct. This puts the rule in conflict with Rule 4.1's legitimization of some deceptive negotiation behaviors, but rules of statutory interpretation give Rule 4.1's specific negotiation analysis precedence over Rule 8.4(c)'s general prohibitions. Nevertheless, Rule 8.4(c)'s straightforward exhortation is more often invoked by bar disciplinary authorities, in part because it augments claims of Rule 4.1 violations.

6. Professor Gerald Wetlaufer has argued against Professor White's view that there are permissible and impermissible lies. Consider the following excerpt:

> For the purposes of this Article, "lying" will be defined to include all means by which one might attempt to create in some audience a belief at variance with one's own. These means include intentional communicative acts, concealments, and omissions. . . .

> It has been suggested that this definition of lying is too broad and that one should, at this early stage of the inquiry, acknowledge a distinction between lying and other lesser deceptions. My reasons for not doing so are three. First, it is perfectly appropriate, at least in American

usage, to define lying as I have done. Second, as is made clear in the new OXFORD ENGLISH DICTIONARY, there is a strong measure of euphemism in our habit of reserving "lying" only for the most serious offenses. This tendency toward euphemism can bring considerable confusion to the inquiry at hand. Third, the desire to distinguish lying from lesser deception rests on the assumption that there is a moral or ethical distinction between these two categories of conduct.

Gerald Wetlaufer, *The Ethics of Lying in Negotiations*, 75 Iowa L. Rev. 1219, 1223 (1990). Who has the better point of view, Professor Wetlaufer or Professor White? Why?

7.   The disagreement between Professors Wetlaufer and White suggests that social norms, the rules of acceptable behavior among individuals in groups or in society at large, are very important in determining what is considered appropriate negotiation behavior. For example, there is a general social norm that lying is wrong and bad, but in the negotiation setting there is a norm allowing for some deception and deceit. This norm, however, is tempered by other factors, such as an individual's comfort level with deceptive behavior and the identity of the recipient of such behavior. Taking these factors into account, Professor G. Richard Shell has identified three sets of norms when it comes to negotiation ethics and identified them as: the Idealist, the Pragmatist, and the Poker Player.

The Idealist views negotiation like any other social setting where people must be held responsible for their actions. Thus, the rules about taking advantage of others apply in the negotiation context, and deception is only acceptable when protecting others from harm or hurt feelings or other similar special situations. Pragmatists take a cost-benefit approach to deception and other questionable tactics and note that the long-term costs associated with them usually outweigh the short-term gains. They also recognize that one's reputation is an important asset, worthy of protecting. Pragmatists may be deceptive with respect to justifications and rationales for offers and counteroffers, which are typically less important to transactions than the substantive matters related to the transaction. Poker Players view deception as an essential element of negotiation, and cunning deceit is to be expected. In this view, an effective negotiator must have a robust distrust of one's counterpart and must engage in hard bargaining tactics when necessary. If a Poker Player has good leverage, the basis for that leverage will be disclosed. And if in a position of lesser or no leverage, Poker Players view bluffing to create an impression of good leverage as critical (much like in a game of poker). G. RICHARD SHELL, BARGAINING FOR ADVANTAGE: NEGOTIATION STRATEGIES FOR REASONABLE PEOPLE 210–214 (2d ed. 2006).

8.   Professor Peter Reilly recommends the following self-help measures to combat a negotiation counterpart's deceit: conducting a thorough background check on the other parties to the negotiation, networking for potential negotiation counterparts, creating rapport, demanding the use of objective standards while avoiding being hamstrung by them, strategically limiting information revelation,

recognizing and thwarting tactics of evasion, establishing long-term relationships and watching for signs of deception, and using "come clean" questions strategically. See Peter Reilly, *Was Machiavelli Right? Lying in Negotiation and the Art of Defensive Self-Help*, 24 Ohio St. J. on Disp. Resol. 481, 525–532 (2010).

B. THE LAW OF BARGAINING

In the following case, we examine in some detail allegations of a lawyer's misrepresentation during litigation-related negotiation. As you read the Minnesota Supreme Court's opinion here, consider how you would have responded to the question asked.

HOYT PROPERTIES, INC. V. PRODUCTION RESOURCE GROUP, L.L.C.
736 N.W.2d 313 (Minn. 2007)

PAGE, JUSTICE.

[In 2001, Hoyt Properties engaged in a multi-million dollar commercial lease with Entolo. When Entolo defaulted, Hoyt filed an unlawful detainer action, and on the day of the eviction hearing Hoyt and Entolo reached a settlement that included a liability release for Entolo's parent corporation, PRG. Hoyt alleges it agreed to the release because of a misrepresentation by PRG's attorneys on the day of the eviction hearing.

According to Hoyt, upon learning that PRG was concerned about being sued after the fact, Hoyt asked, "I don't know of any reason how we could pierce the veil, do you?" Hoyt alleges that PRG's attorney responded, "There isn't anything. PRG and Entolo are totally separate." However, Hoyt later learned of a lawsuit brought by a third party against Entolo that alleged breach of contract by Entolo but sought to hold its parent company, PRG, liable by piercing the corporate veil. The complaint alleged, among other things, that Entolo failed to observe corporate formalities, was operated by PRG as a division rather than a separate corporation, and was undercapitalized by PRG.

Hoyt filed this action to rescind the settlement agreement and to pierce the corporate veil to hold PRG liable for Entolo's breach of the lease. Hoyt alleges the PRG representations were false and that the attorney either knew or should have known that the representations were false.]

* * *

When reviewing a grant of summary judgment, we review the record to determine: "(1) whether there are any genuine issues of material fact for trial; and (2) whether the trial court erred in its application of the law." We review the evidence in the light most favorable to the nonmoving party, in this case, Hoyt.

To make out a claim for fraudulent misrepresentation, the plaintiff must establish that:

> (1) there was a false representation by a party of a past or existing material fact susceptible of knowledge; (2) made with knowledge of the falsity of the representation or made as of the party's own knowledge without knowing whether it was true or false; (3) with the intention to induce another to act in reliance thereon; (4) that the representation caused the other party to act in reliance thereon; and (5) that the party suffer[ed] pecuniary damage as a result of the reliance.

Appellants argue that the statements at issue do not amount to statements of past or present material fact as required under the first prong of our fraudulent misrepresentation standard.

As the court of appeals noted, abstract statements of law or pure legal opinions are not actionable; however, a mixed statement of law and fact may be actionable "if it amounts to an implied assertion that facts exist that justify the conclusion of law which is expressed" and the other party would ordinarily have no knowledge of the facts. . . . Thus, according to the Restatement, one who says, " 'I think that my title to this land is good, but do not take my word for it; consult your own lawyer,' " cannot be reasonably understood as asserting any fact with respect to the title. However, a legal statement in the form of an expression of opinion may still be actionable if it carries "with it by implication the assertion that the facts known to the maker are not incompatible with his opinion or that he does know facts that justify him in forming it." For example, a statement that one mortgage has priority over another may imply an assertion that one was made before the other; and a statement that a corporation has the legal right to do business in a state may carry with it an assurance that it has as a matter of fact taken all of the steps necessary to be duly qualified.

In order to evaluate the statement at issue in this case, it is helpful to review the standard courts use to determine whether to pierce the corporate veil. A court may pierce the corporate veil to hold a shareholder liable for the debts of the corporation when the shareholder is the alter ego of the corporation. When using the alter ego theory to pierce the corporate veil, courts look to the "reality and not form, with how the corporation operated and the individual defendant's relationship to that operation." Factors relevant to that inquiry include insufficient capitalization for purposes of corporate undertaking, failure to observe corporate formalities, nonpayment of dividends, insolvency of debtor corporation at time of transaction in question, siphoning of funds by dominant shareholder, nonfunctioning of other officers and directors, absence of corporate records, and existence of corporation as merely facade for individual dealings.

Appellants assert that the representations PRG's attorney allegedly made were statements of the attorney's legal opinion only and thus were not actionable. Appellants argue that Steve Hoyt's question, "I don't know of any reason how we could pierce the veil, do you?," solicited the view of PRG's attorney regarding a legal claim, to which PRG's attorney responded with the legal opinion "There isn't anything." As to the second part of the alleged representation, "PRG and Entolo are totally separate," appellants argue that this was also a legal opinion, and that the word "separate" is a legal term of art that "does not describe a particular factual predicate in a piercing-the-veil case, but rather, a general legal conclusion that piercing is not warranted." Hoyt asserts that the representation that "There isn't anything" "implied that PRG's and Entolo's business operations justified [the attorney's] conclusion that there was not 'anything' to a good-faith piercing claim" and that the representation that "PRG and Entolo are totally separate" was a direct factual statement bolstering the assertion that there were no facts supporting a veil-piercing claim. Hoyt further asserts that Steve Hoyt had no knowledge of the facts underlying PRG's corporate relationship with Haas and Entolo.

. . . When viewed in the light most favorable to Hoyt, as is required under the summary judgment standard, the representation "There isn't anything" is a representation that no facts exist that would support a piercing claim against PRG—for example, no facts indicating that Entolo did not maintain corporate formalities. Even if we assume, as appellants argue, that the alleged statement made by PRG's attorney was an expression of his legal opinion, that representation implies that the attorney was aware of facts supporting that opinion, namely, that there were no facts to support a claim to pierce the corporate veil. Because the representation was not an expression of pure legal opinion (for example, "I do not think someone could pierce the veil but I am not sure"), but rather a statement implying that facts existed that supported a legal opinion, we conclude that the representation is actionable.

We conclude that the second alleged representation, "PRG and Entolo are totally separate," is also actionable. Again viewed in the light most favorable to Hoyt, the second representation constitutes a direct factual assertion that the relationship between PRG and Entolo is such that no facts exist that would allow the corporate veil to be pierced; for example, that no facts existed that would demonstrate that Entolo was a façade for PRG's own dealings. As such, it is the kind of representation that we have traditionally held to be actionable.

* * *

The record is sufficient for us to conclude that there are also genuine issues of material fact for trial as to whether PRG's attorney made the representations at issue without knowing whether they were true or false. . . . In his deposition, PRG's attorney also admitted that when he made the alleged representations at issue he had not yet formed an opinion, one way or the other, about the facts alleged in the complaint. Given these admissions, a finder of fact could conclude that when PRG's attorney responded to Steve Hoyt's question he did not know whether his representations were true. As such, there is a genuine issue of material fact for trial as to whether he made the representations "without knowing whether [they were] true or false."

III.

Finally, we address the district court's finding that "Hoyt's reliance on opposing counsel's remarks was unreasonable as a matter of law." . . . To prevail on a claim of fraudulent misrepresentation, the complaining party must set forth evidence demonstrating both actual and reasonable reliance. . . . To establish actual reliance, Hoyt offered Steve Hoyt's deposition testimony that he agreed to release PRG from liability because he relied on the representations PRG's attorney made regarding piercing the corporate veil. On this record, Steve Hoyt's testimony is sufficient to defeat summary judgment on the question of actual reliance. . . .

Because we hold that Hoyt established genuine issues of material fact for trial as to the required elements of a fraudulent misrepresentation claim, we affirm the court of appeals' decision and remand to the district court for further proceedings.

Affirmed.

ANDERSON, PAUL H., JUSTICE (dissenting).

I respectfully dissent.

* * *

The first element of a claim for fraudulent misrepresentation is only met if the false factual representation by the party involves a "fact susceptible of knowledge." When this standard is applied to the facts in this case, it is difficult to see how PRG's attorney's representations can be actionable. First, in order for PRG's attorney to imply facts that "[t]here isn't anything" to a veil-piercing claim, the attorney would have to imply a factual assertion that the second prong of the claim is met—that the claim is "necessary to avoid injustice or fundamental unfairness." Because this is a subjective inquiry made by a court, it is not a "fact susceptible of knowledge," and even if it was, it is unreasonable to conclude that PRG's attorney falsely implied that a veil-piercing claim in this case would not meet this prong. In other words, if PRG's attorney was to evaluate the claim and decide that it was viable, the attorney would have to conclude that it would be unjust and fundamentally unfair for the attorney's client to escape liability. Those are not the type of conclusions we can expect, or even desire, a legal advocate to make, and they are generally not susceptible of the attorney's knowledge.

* * *

In light of Steve Hoyt's extensive legal and business background, his documented practice of relying on his own legal counsel in his business practices, and his standard lease clause advising others to do the same, I conclude that on this record, Hoyt Properties fails to establish reasonable reliance on PRG's attorney's statements as a matter of law. Steve Hoyt's bare assertions that "lawyers [in this city] are pretty forthright and honest" and "have a duty to tell the truth" are not legally sufficient to establish a genuine issue of material fact regarding reasonable reliance. Therefore, I conclude that Hoyt Properties cannot establish the fourth element of fraudulent misrepresentation.

Finally, I also share the policy concerns of amicus curiae Minnesota Defense Lawyers Association that the majority's decision will have the adverse effect of discouraging settlement among parties, based on a lack of confidence in the enforceability of settlement agreements. Fewer settlement agreements could create further demands on the court system and also create additional risk and expense for parties in litigation. Further, I am concerned that what the majority has done with its opinion is to design a roadmap with a well-defined exit route for parties who experience remorse after entering into a settlement agreement. . . .

POINTS FOR DISCUSSION

1.   As *Hoyt Properties* illustrates, it can be difficult to determine whether a representation is one of fact or opinion. Comment d to Section 525 of the RESTATEMENT (SECOND) OF TORTS (1977) provides:

> Strictly speaking, "fact" includes not only the existence of a tangible thing or the happening of a particular event or the relationship between particular persons or things, but also the state of mind, such as the entertaining of an intention or the holding of an opinion, of any person, whether the maker of a representation or a third person. Indeed, every assertion of the existence of a thing is a representation of the speaker's state of mind, namely, his belief in its existence. There is sometimes, however, a marked difference between what constitutes justifiable reliance upon statements of the maker's opinion and what constitutes justifiable reliance upon other representations. Therefore, it is convenient to distinguish between misrepresentations of opinion and misrepresentations of all other facts, including intention.

> A statement of law may have the effect of a statement of fact or a statement of opinion. It has the effect of a statement of fact if it asserts that a particular statute has been enacted or repealed or that a particular decision has been rendered upon particular facts. It has the effect of a statement of opinion if it expresses only the actor's judgment as to the legal consequence that would be attached to the particular state of facts if the question were litigated. It is therefore convenient to deal separately with misrepresentations of law.

2.   Likewise, the RESTATEMENT (SECOND) OF CONTRACTS (1981) deals with misrepresentations, providing that they can both prevent contract formation and make a contract voidable.

§ 163 When a Misrepresentation Prevents the Formation of a Contract

If a misrepresentation as to the character or essential terms of a proposed contract induces conduct that appears to be a manifestation of assent by one who neither knows nor has reasonable opportunity to know of the character or essential terms of the proposed contract, his conduct is not effective as a manifestation of assent.

§ 164 When a Misrepresentation Makes a Contract Voidable

(1)   If a party's manifestation of assent is induced by either fraudulent or material misrepresentation by the other party upon which the recipient is justified in relying, the contract is voidable by the recipient.

While the difference between whether a contract is void or voidable may seem small, misrepresentations in negotiation can lead to very serious consequences including criminal liability for fraudulent misrepresentations involving both restitution and jail time.

3.   Misrepresentation is not the only common law action that lawyer negotiators need to be wary of. For example, improper bargaining pressure on weaker parties can give rise to claims of duress or undue influence during contract formation. Duress results from two categories of threats, (a) physical threats forcing a party to enter into a contract and (b) threats of criminal conduct, wrongful seizure or retention of goods, or legal process leaving no reasonable alternative to entering into a contract. Typical bargaining stress and pressure associated with leverage such as refusing future dealings or hard bargaining between experienced counterparts are not the kind of threats contemplated by duress. See RESTATEMENT (SECOND) OF CONTRACTS § 176 (1981). Undue influence, on the other hand, occurs when a person in a trusted role or position exploits that trust to unfairly manipulate the other's judgment when deciding whether to enter into a contract. It is not necessary for the trusted person to benefit from the use of his or her influence. The typical remedy for duress and undue influence victims is rescission of the contract as opposed to an affirmative claim for damages. See *id.* § 177. See generally ART HINSHAW, NEGOTIATION ETHICS, IN 1 THE NEGOTIATOR'S DESK REFERENCE (Andrea Kupfer Schneider & Christopher Honeyman eds., 2017).

> **Negotiation Nugget**
> For more on the law of bargaining see Russell Korobkin, Michael Moffitt, and Nancy Welsh, *The Law of Bargaining*, 87 Marq. L. Rev. 839 (2004).

4.   In the U.S., parties have no common legal obligation to negotiate in good faith to reach a final agreement. There are some statutory exceptions, most notably in the collective bargaining context. For example, the National Labor Relations Act imposes a duty on labor and management to bargain in "good faith." Determining what is and is not good faith is difficult, and typically comes down to a list of actions and tactics that are prohibited, such as disengaging from negotiations within a certain time frame or presenting take-it-or-leave-it offers. In addition, parties may enter into a binding agreement expressing their commitment to negotiate in good faith. A cause of action for breach of the duty to negotiate in good faith therefore requires the following showings: 1) both parties manifested an intention to be bound by an agreement to negotiate in good faith; 2) the terms of the agreement are sufficiently definite to be enforced; and 3) consideration was conferred. See *Flight Sys., Inc. v. Elec. Data Sys. Corp.*, 112 F.3d 124, 130 (3d Cir. 1997), *Bennett v. Itochu Int'l Inc.*, 682 F. Supp. 2d 469 (E.D. Pa. 2010) (finding that "non-binding" term sheet nonetheless conferred a bargained-for benefit and was sufficient to give rise to duty to negotiate in good faith).

5. Professor Michael Moffitt argues that current malpractice actions focus too heavily on lawyer-as-litigator instead of lawyer-as-settlor concepts. Although the vast majority of legal actions settle, only:

> **Negotiation Nugget**
>
> For an in-depth discussion of the negotiation issues surrounding plea bargaining, see Cynthia Alkon, *Plea Bargaining: An Example of Negotiating with Constraints*, in The Negotiator's Desk Reference 683 (Chris Honeyman & Andrea Kupfer Schneider eds., 2017).

1 percent of reported legal malpractice cases and only about 1.5 percent of bar complaints relate to lawyers' roles in settlement. . . . Instead, the realities of modern lawyering, in which the lawyer-as-settlor role is more prominent, demand that lawyers be held to a different set of standards than those created solely with litigation in mind. . . . The advice lawyers provide to their clients about the prospect of settlement does not deserve the sweeping judgmental deference of lawyers' litigation decisions. . . . Clients' ability to exercise autonomy—the ability to choose between settlement and continued litigation—should be recognized in practice, not just in the theoretical or aspirational standards of the profession.

Michael Moffitt, *Settlement Malpractice*, 86 Univ. of Chicago L. Rev. 1825, 1893 (2019).

6. Although our primary focus is on lawyers' involvement in negotiating civil litigation settlement and transactions, lawyers also negotiate constantly in the criminal context. And, not surprisingly, claims of coercion also arise in connection with plea bargaining. The seminal case in this area is *Brady v. United States*, 397 U.S. 742 (1970). Brady holds that when a defendant negotiates a guilty plea and thus waives the constitutional right to trial, such waiver "not only must be voluntary but must be [a] knowing, intelligent act[ ] done with sufficient awareness of the relevant circumstances and likely consequences." *Id.* at 748.

CHAPTER 6

DIFFERENCES AMONG NEGOTIATORS

As we have already mentioned, negotiators often make assumptions about the motives and goals of their negotiation counterparts. Sometimes these assumptions are grounded in substantial experience in negotiating with that person or others who seem similar to her. In other cases, these assumptions are grounded in stereotypes, which themselves may be based on substantial (or limited) experience or commonly held understandings about characteristics of people who belong to a certain social identity group.

At times, these stereotypes will prove useful; at other times, however, they will mislead. There is a growing amount of scholarly work on culture and conflict. There is also a growing recognition of the extent and effects of implicit bias and unconscious bias. See, e.g., Anthony G. Greenwald & Linda Hamilton Krieger, *Implicit Bias: Scientific Foundations*, 94 Cal. L. Rev. 945 (2006); Debra Lyn Bassett, *Deconstruct and Superstruct: Examining Bias Across the Legal System*, 46 U.C. Davis L. Rev. 1563 (2013). Recall our earlier discussion about the mental shortcuts, or heuristics, that we rely upon so frequently. Recall, too, our discussion of the frequently negative effects of cognitive biases and the fundamental attribution error.

We cannot, and perhaps would not even want to try to, offer here an exhaustive catalogue of the values, strategies and techniques that could characterize negotiators from different cultures or social identities. Rather, we will focus on helping you to develop a way to think about these issues in negotiation. We begin by suggesting the overwhelming importance of approaching these topics with humility and open-mindedness. We can only learn from and about each other if we are willing to listen.

A. CULTURE

"Culture" is not a simple concept. In the following reading, Professor Jayne Seminare Docherty, an anthropologist, describes three different ways of thinking about culture and negotiation. Moving from what she considers to be the least sophisticated to the most sophisticated, these three approaches are the "tip of the iceberg" approach, the "patterns" approach, and the "symmetrical anthropology" approach. After we consider each of these in turn, we will then explore subcultures.

JAYNE SEMINARE DOCHERTY, CULTURE AND NEGOTIATION:
SYMMETRICAL ANTHROPOLOGY FOR NEGOTIATORS
87 Marq. L. Rev. 711, 712–717 (2004)

Unfortunately, some negotiation texts—particularly but not exclusively popular books on negotiation—focus almost entirely on the part of the iceberg visible above the surface. In these texts, cultures are presented as lists of do's and don'ts. These lists are rooted in stereotypes and are of dubious value. Teaching negotiators about culture in this manner is of limited value and might actually be dangerous in some settings.

* * *

A more sophisticated approach to culture in negotiation involves identifying patterns or types of cultures by studying a large group of cultures. Instead of getting inside of a specific culture to understand it, this approach stands outside of cultures and looks for patterns or cultural styles. These are often presented as a list of dichotomous characteristics including: high context/low context; individualism/collectivism; and egalitarian/ hierarchical. A high-context culture often relies on indirect communication, because the participants are expected to understand the complex meaning of relatively small non-verbal gestures. A low-context culture will tend to rely on direct statements and formal, clear ratification of written negotiated agreements. Negotiators from individualist cultures may worry less about preserving relationships than negotiators from collectivist cultures. And, negotiators from egalitarian cultures are likely to be less concerned about issues of rank and privilege than negotiators from hierarchical cultures.

* * *

The most complete and sophisticated way of thinking about culture and negotiation requires that we greatly enrich our definition of culture. Avruch offers the following definition: "For our purposes, culture refers to the socially transmitted values, beliefs and symbols that are more or less shared by members of a social group, and by means of which members interpret and make meaningful their experience and behavior (including the behavior of 'others')." He also points out that this definition includes a number of assumptions. First, individuals belong to multiple groups and therefore carry multiple cultures. The implication is that an encounter between two individuals is likely to be a multicultural encounter since each participant can draw on more than one culture to make sense of the situation. This includes negotiation encounters. Second, it is important to understand the institutions and mechanisms that transmit culture. Third, culture is almost never perfectly shared by all members of a community or group. Individuals have the capacity to selectively adopt and adapt their multiple cultures, so you cannot assume that a person from culture X will do Y. Each party can draw from, adapt, and modify a multifaceted set of cultural norms and rules; therefore every intercultural encounter is a complex improvisational experience.

It is critically important to remember that our own cultures are largely invisible to us; they are simply our "common sense" understandings of the world. Hence, "conflict is, at essence, the construction of a special type of reality. Most of the time we assume and take for granted that we share a single reality with others, but we do not." We see culture when we are forced to recognize that not everyone experiences and lives in the world the way we do. Perhaps we experience "language shock" when we recognize that someone may be speaking the same language, but we are not sure they live on the same planet we do. Or, we may encounter someone whose "moral order"—their "pattern of . . . compulsions and permissions to act in certain ways and [their] prohibitions against acting in other ways"— differs from our own. In negotiations, these moments of shock and surprise may occur around issues of risk because risk is very much a cultural construct. We may also experience surprise when people use the same language, even the same metaphors, but we discover that their shared language is actually covering over profound differences in their sense of reality. What we assume is negotiable may not be negotiable to another person and vice versa.

> **Note**
>
> Professor Kimberlé Crenshaw coined the term intersectionality in 1989 to describe the way overlapping social identities do not fit conventional ways of understanding inequalities or disadvantages. See Demarginalizing the Intersection of Race and Sex: A Black Feminist Critique of Antidiscrimination Doctrine, Feminist Theory and Antiracist Politics, 1989 U. Chi. Legal F. 139.

As negotiators, the recognition that we have a culture too reshapes the reality within which we work. We are forced to grapple with the fact that the very domain of our work—social conflict—is culturally constructed.

* * *

When we encounter cultural differences about when and how to negotiate, we can focus on what the other person is doing "wrong" compared to us. . . . Or, instead of focusing on what is wrong with the other culture, we can become adept at a form of "symmetrical anthropology" that is "capable of confronting not beliefs that do not touch us directly—we are always

critical enough of them—but the true knowledge to which we adhere totally."
We can subject our own culture(s) to the same scrutiny we apply to the
culture(s) of others. That means we will need to become critically aware of
our own assumptions about negotiation. What does it mean to say "get
beneath positions to interests?" Does everyone share the assumptions about
human nature and social relationships on which this approach to finding a
"win-win" solution rests?

POINTS FOR DISCUSSION

1.   Professor Docherty refers to three dichotomies that researchers have
studied: high-context versus low-context, individualist versus collectivist, and
egalitarian versus hierarchical. Researchers categorize the United States as low-
context, individualist, and egalitarian.

2.   Professor Docherty offers several suggestions to those who would like to
improve their skills as "symmetrical anthropologists," including broadening one's
expectations, attempting to understand our own and others' worldviews, and
exploring the metaphors that people embroiled in conflict use in their speech.

3.   How might one handle cultural differences in negotiation? Consider the
following suggestion:

> **Negotiation Nugget**
>
> For an in-depth discussion
> on culture and negotiation
> see Jeanne M. Brett,
> NEGOTIATING GLOBALLY
> (2001).

First, while cultural/national
boundaries clearly do exist, much of
what passes for such differences may
well be the result of expectations and
perceptions which, when acted upon,
help to bring about a form of self-
fulfilling prophecy. Perhaps the best
way to combat such expectations is
to go out of one's way to acquire as
much information as one can
beforehand about the way people in
other cultures view the kind of problem under consideration. Thus, if we
are negotiating with a German about a health care contract, we should try
to find out whatever we can about how Germans tend to view health care.
Of course, in large countries, there may be regional variations that also
need to be taken into account. Second, it is important to enter into such
negotiations with self-conscious awareness of the powerful tendency we
share toward stereotyping; this kind of consciousness-raising may, in its
own right, help make it a bit less likely that we will slip into a set of

perceptual biases that over-determine what transpires in the negotiations proper.

Third, it is important to enter into negotiations across cultural/national lines by trying to give your counterpart the (cultural) benefit of the doubt. Just as you would not wish others to assume that you are nothing more than an exemplar of people from your culture, try similarly to avoid making the same mistaken assumption about the other person.

Jeffrey Z. Rubin & Frank E.A. Sander, *Culture, Negotiation, and the Eye of the Beholder*, 7 Negot. J. 249, 252 (1991).

4.   Cultures may be divided further into subcultures, which can be quite different within a single culture. For example, if we assume that there is a national culture within the United States, there are still different regional subcultures that can be extraordinarily important from a conflict and negotiation perspective. For example, how would you describe the differences between the cultures of New York, Los Angeles, St. Louis, and Atlanta? Or between a big city and small town in your state? How might these cultural differences impact legal negotiations?

5.   Religion provides another example of the culture/subculture phenomenon. Jeffrey Seul observes, "Religion offers much more to individuals and groups in their effort to construct and maintain secure identities than do most other social institutions, so religion is often at the core of individuals'—and groups'—conceptions of themselves." Jeffrey R. Seul, Religion and Conflict, in THE NEGOTIATOR'S FIELDBOOK: THE DESK REFERENCE FOR THE EXPERIENCED NEGOTIATOR 323, 325 (Andrea Kupfer Schneider & Christopher Honeyman eds., 2006). How might religious differences impact legal negotiations?

B.   GENDER

A negotiator's gender may also play a role in negotiation. The following excerpt highlights the behavior (and perceptions of behavior) of women who negotiate as lawyers and other professionals. As you read this excerpt, consider whether, in your experience, the assertions made ring true.

CARRIE MENKEL-MEADOW, WHAT DIFFERENCE DOES "GENDER DIFFERENCE" MAKE?
18 Disp. Resol. Mag. 4, 5–7 (2012)

This essay reviews some of the continuing efforts to determine whether gender has any significant or predicable impact on dispute resolution behavior. I continue to think this is an interesting, but inconclusive question, especially because dispute resolution is itself an interactive process involving parties, representatives (lawyers) and dispute resolvers or facilitators (negotiators, mediators, arbitrators and judges, among other roles), so that the mix or context of gendered participants interact with each other and also with the site (court, private mediation, quasi-private arbitration, negotiation) and subject matter of any particular dispute. Although I continue to think that gender somehow matters, sometimes, in some places, more recent research indicates that the difference that gender difference makes is quite variable, depending on case type, context, role of participant (e.g., agent or principal) and now perhaps, different generations of disputants and disputes.

* * *

Professionals in Dispute Resolution: Lawyers and Other Representatives

Carol Gilligan's work in the 1980s produced many studies seeking to discern if there were gender differences in different professions, especially the legal profession, and in different decision-making contexts. One of her students studied differences in ethical decision-making by male and female lawyers and learned that when lawyer ethical rules were relatively clear, there were little to no differences in how male and female lawyers decided what was ethically mandated. But when the rules were more ambiguous, such as whether to turn over adverse evidence to a lawyer on the other side of a case, or when actual harm to a person was involved, such as custody issues for children, women lawyers were slightly more likely to consider "justice" to the other side, rather than "pure" zealous advocacy. Later studies by Gilligan have demonstrated some merging of gender differences, that is, more girls moving to the male (clearer "justice" rule-based) mode of decision-making, while a smaller core of girls and young women remain committed to a "care" and relational approach to moral decision making and problem solving, though studies also demonstrate that newer generations engage in more "cross-over" or context specific forms of reasoning.

Earlier work on women in business and other professional settings demonstrates that to the extent women have something particular or different to offer, there must be a "critical mass" (variable in different sectors) for the message to be accepted on its own merits and be "detached" from a gendered representation. Studies of both law students in negotiation classes and now a few of lawyers confirm that negotiated outcomes do not differ by gender. But perceptions of results achieved (e.g., women are more self-doubting and critical, are more likely to take negotiation courses pass/fail) or assumptions that stereotypic behavior is expected continue to document differences between perceptions and assumptions and the actual outcomes and behaviors in negotiation.

Of the more recent studies on lawyer behavior, particularly in the mediation setting, Relis suggests that women lawyers, particularly defense counsel in medical malpractice cases, had greater "extra-legal sensitivity" (the need for non-compensatory items, like apologies, etc.) and concern for parties on the other side of cases than did male attorneys. But Relis also found that more facilitative female mediators, especially non-lawyer mediators, tended to be overpowered by aggressive male litigators in mediation settings, suggesting that some of the earlier observed gender differences are not yet gone. Relis' study also found that female plaintiffs were more likely to be overpowered by male mediators during mediations than male plaintiffs, demonstrating that the interaction of the gender of the party, lawyer or representative and dispute manager professional (mediator or judge) is complex. It often involves, as Relis eloquently states, "differentially experienced parallel worlds" in mediation by parties, lawyers and mediators, where gender differential is still part of the experience.

POINTS FOR DISCUSSION

1.   We use generalizations to simplify a complicated world. In this regard, generalizations are second cousins to the stereotypes, cognitive biases, and heuristics introduced throughout this book. As you have seen, and will continue to see, these sorts of "mental shortcuts" are inevitable, sometimes useful, and sometimes very dangerous. Available empirical research has explored the generalization that certain categories of people are more likely than others to recognize and grasp opportunities for negotiation. The people who recognize and grasp these opportunities tend to do better. Professor Linda Babcock and Sara Laschever examine this phenomenon through the prism of gender:

> Could it be that women don't get more of the things they want in life in part because they don't think to ask for them? Are there external pressures that discourage women from asking as much as men do—and even keep them from realizing what they can ask? Are women really less likely than men to ask for what they want?

> To explore this question, Linda conducted a study that looked at the starting salaries of students graduating from Carnegie Mellon University with their master's degrees. When Linda looked exclusively at gender, the difference was fairly large: The starting salaries of the men were 7.6 percent or almost $4,000 higher on average than those of the women. Trying to explain this difference, Linda looked next at who had negotiated his or her salary (who had asked for more money) and who had simply accepted the initial offer he or she had received. It turned out that only 7

percent of the female students had negotiated but 57 percent (eight times as many) of the men had asked for more money.

Linda was particularly surprised to find such a dramatic difference between men and women at Carnegie Mellon because graduating students are strongly advised by the school's Career Services department to negotiate their job offers. Nonetheless, hardly any of the women had done so. The most striking finding, however, was that the students who had negotiated (most of them men) were able to increase their starting salaries by 7.4 percent on average, or $4,053—almost exactly the difference between men's and women's average starting pay. This suggests that the salary differences between the men and the women might have been eliminated if the women had negotiated their offers.

LINDA BABCOCK & SARA LASCHEVER, WOMEN DON'T ASK: NEGOTIATION AND THE GENDER DIVIDE, 1–2 (2003). In a subsequent laboratory experiment designed to study propensity to negotiate, Professor Babcock and two colleagues, Deborah Small and Michele Gelfand, found that "almost nine times as many male as female subjects asked for more money." LINDA BABCOCK AND SARA LASCHEVER, WOMEN DON'T ASK: THE HIGH COST OF AVOIDING NEGOTIATION AND POSITIVE STRATEGIES FOR CHANGE, 2–3 (2007). Two subsequent studies suggested that men initiate four times as many negotiations as women. The lesson? Regardless of any of your sources of social identity, it is important to ask for what you want.

> **Negotiation Nugget**
>
> For an interesting take on women and negotiation, see Andrea Schneider, Women Don't Negotiate and Other Similar Nonsense, TEDx, https://www.youtube.com/watch?time_continue=5&v=jFX1wAOv724.

> **Negotiation Nugget**
>
> For Professor Schneider's take on men and negotiation see Gender and Negotiation: What About the Guys? https://law.unlv.edu/webcast/2018-chris-beecroft-lecture-andrea-schneider.

2. A recent meta-analysis found "small and highly variable" gender differences in negotiation and important contextual differences that influenced the outcomes obtained by men and women. The authors situate these contextual differences within research on gender roles, suggesting that "women who deviate from the female role—for instance by acting assertively—risk incurring *social backlash*." The researchers further stated, "Notably, the results revealed a bargaining advantage for men under conditions of highest predicted

role incongruity for women (when negotiators are not experienced, in negotiations with high structural ambiguity, and [when negotiators are bargaining on behalf of themselves]), but a bargaining advantage for women under conditions of lowest predicted role incongruity (when they possess negotiation experience, are negotiating for an individual, and [in negotiations with low structural ambiguity])." Jens Mazei, Joachim Hüffmeier, Philipp Alexander Freund, Alice F. Stuhlmacher, Lena Bilke & Guido Hertal, *A Meta-Analysis on Gender Differences in Negotiation Outcomes and Their Moderators,* 141 Psychol. Bull. 85, 85–86 & 94 (2015).

3.   The Mazei, et al. study looked at 51 separate studies of gender and negotiation that compared and reported final economic outcomes achieved by women and men in actual negotiation tasks in which economic outcomes could be achieved, such as salary negotiations. Only two of the 51 studies were of lawyers— or more precisely of law students. Does this make the study's conclusions irrelevant to lawyers? Professor Charles B. Craver has kept copious records of the outcomes of his law students' negotiation results throughout his career. He reports:

> Since 1973, I have taught Legal Negotiation courses in which we study the negotiation process and the factors that influence bargaining interactions. . . . Over the past thirty-five years, I have performed several statistical analyses of student negotiation performance based upon gender. I have found absolutely no statistically significant differences between the results achieved by men and by women. The average results are almost identical.

CHARLES B. CRAVER, LEGAL NEGOTIATING: SKILLS AND VALUES 143 (2d ed. 2012). Why do you think Professor Craver obtained a different result from the Mazei, et al., study?

4.   Based on Professor Andrea Schneider's empirical study of negotiators in Chicago and Milwaukee, Professor Schneider and her colleagues suggest, consistent with results of the Mazei, et al. study discussed in note 2, that when women lawyers are negotiating on behalf of their clients, they are significantly less likely to confront the effects of social backlash. Andrea Kupfer Schneider, Catherine H. Tinsley, Sandra Cheldelin & Emily T. Amanatullah, *Likeability v. Competence: The Impossible Choice Faced by Female Politicians, Attenuated by Lawyers,* 17 Duke J. Gender L. & Pol'y 363, 364 (2010). The coauthors also provide advice for female lawyers in other contexts where social backlash may be more salient. *See also* Laura J. Kray, *Leading Through Negotiation: Harnessing the Power of Gender Stereotypes,* 50 Cal. Mgmt. Rev. 159 (2007); Andrea Schneider, *Negotiating While Female,* 70 SMU L. Rev. 695 (2017).

5.   What should a woman, a man, or anyone do when they encounter identity-based stereotypes and offensive behavior? Professor Andrea Schneider suggests four types of responses a negotiator can make to an offensive comment— ignoring, confronting, deflecting, and engaging. Ignoring, simply disregarding the comment, and confronting, challenging the statement, are at opposite ends on the

spectrum of possible responses. Deflecting means acknowledging the statement and moving on, while engaging means having an open conversation about the speaker's purpose in making the remark and your feelings upon hearing it. Not surprisingly, engaging can be the most difficult as it requires checking your assumptions about the speaker's intentions by asking what their purpose was in making the comment. After the speaker responds, you can gather additional data about intentions and ask further questions. Professor Schneider believes that engaging is the most advantageous response as it focuses on understanding in a nonconfrontational and nonthreatening manner. In addition, such engagement does not have to happen immediately; it can be done at a later date. See Andrea Schneider, *Effective Responses to Offensive Comments*, 10 Negot. J. 107, 111–113 (1994).

   6.   Many people believe that ethical decision making is affected by one's gender, and most of the studies on the topic find either that women act more ethically than men or there is no difference. Professors Leigh Thompson and Jason Pierce conducted a series of experiments that found men were more competitive than women in negotiations (and tended to lie more) and women were more empathetic than men (and lied less). However, when Professors Thompson and Pierce framed the negotiations in a more competitive context, women became more competitive (and lied almost as much as the men). Similarly, when they framed the negotiation in a more empathetic context, men become more collaborative (and lied less). Leigh Thompson, *Simple Prompts Can Get Women to Negotiate More Like Men, and Vice Versa*, Harv. Bus. Rev. (September 17, 2018). Professors Art Hinshaw and Jess Alberts also looked at gender as a part of a much larger study of negotiation ethics. The study focused on a client's request to his lawyer to engage in a fraudulent negotiation scheme to settle a claim in clear violation of Rule 4.1 of the Model Rules of Professional Conduct. They found no difference in the responses of male and female lawyers when asked to engage in the fraudulent strategy, but they did find a difference in a follow-up request to engage in an omission strategy that also violated Rule 4.1. Male lawyers refused this request at a higher rate than did female lawyers (68% compared to 53%), and female lawyers were more likely to indicate that they would engage in the omission strategy than male lawyers (18% compared to 12%). Interestingly, Hinshaw and Alberts found that professional experience played a part in this result as female lawyers with less than 10 years of legal experience were least likely to refuse the request and most likely to agree to the request as compared to male or female lawyers with 10–19 years of experience and 20 or more years of experience. What might explain this difference? See Art Hinshaw & Jess K. Alberts, *Gender and Attorney Negotiation Ethics*, 39 Wash. U. J.L. & Pol'y 145, 162–166 (2012).

C.   RACE

   Like culture and gender, reactions to a negotiator's race may influence negotiation behavior. The following excerpt by Professor Michael Green describes the results of several studies that have explored the effects of race on negotiation outcomes.

MICHAEL Z. GREEN, NEGOTIATING WHILE BLACK

in THE NEGOTIATOR'S DESK REFERENCE 563, 563–581
(Christopher Honeyman and Andrea Kupfer Schneider, eds. 2017)

Looking at all the difficult experiences for a black person in our society . . . one could easily view most transactions as not fitting the platitudes espoused in the dispute resolution community about resolving disputes in a creative way and expanding the pie beyond a zero-sum game. Rather, to be black and negotiating a transaction, chances are the black person may perceive the negotiation process as a game where the black person involved is merely a pawn destined to lose the game. . . . In reviewing the studies that capture what it is to be negotiating while black, one can better understand the realities of this problem even if negotiation theorists have rarely addressed this subject in any comprehensive and prescriptive manner. For decades, commentators have raised concerns about the prejudice involved with informal dispute resolution processes. Cynthia Mabry expresses these concerns for blacks in negotiations as far back as 1998.

> Empirical studies have shown that race affects negotiations. For example, when adversaries are members of the same race, they bargain more cooperatively with one another. Same-race disputants are more cooperative because they trust each other more easily than they trust people of different racial groups. In contrast, intercultural adversaries endeavor to 'maintain a certain face or posture in the eyes of someone different.' This posturing influences the parties' efforts to solve their problem.

* * *

[T]he most prominent studies of race in negotiation while being black were conducted by Ian Ayres, now at Yale Law School. . . . Unlike any other scholar in this field, Ayres used testers as the groundwork for assessing the implications of negotiation based on race. In a 1991 study, with one report in 1991 and further analysis from a new and expanded audit of that study with resulting data and conclusions reported in 1995, Ayres examined differences based upon race by using pairs of testers, always including a white male versus someone of a different race, who were all trained to negotiate the same way and sent to purchase a new car at randomly-selected Chicago auto dealerships. Overall, Ayres found that black buyers were induced to pay much higher prices due to both the initial offer they received from the salesperson and also the final offer which represented the lowest price offered by the salesperson after a number of rounds of bargaining. Specific results demonstrated that "[b]lack female testers were asked to pay over three times the mark-up of white male testers, and black male testers were asked to pay over twice the white male markup." Ayres also found that salespersons believed that white males had better search details and were more informed about the dealer's actual costs than black purchasers. The Ayres studies did not address discrimination in automobile loan financing because the script for those testers required that they inform the dealerships that the testers would provide their own financing.

Twenty years later and with similar concerns about fair negotiations of car purchases by blacks (but this time with respect to loan financing), the United States Department of Justice (DOJ) brought a federal court action against "Japanese automaker Honda [who] agreed to pay $25 million to settle US claims that it discriminated against minority buyers by overcharging them for auto loans." The DOJ asserted that Honda had charged higher interest rates on car loans based on race rather than purchasers' "creditworthiness or other objective criteria related to borrower risk." Although Honda denied it had discriminated, in the July 2015 settlement Honda agreed to give $24 million to be used to compensate purchasers who had allegedly been subjected to discrimination, and an additional one million dollars for consumer education programs. The DOJ and the Consumer Financial Protection Board (CFPB) alleged that Honda dealers made black borrowers pay $250 more per auto loan than white borrowers. Even before this Honda case, researchers had established that blacks "receive higher interest rates on car loans obtained from car dealers than similarly situated white borrowers...while those who receive loans directly from banks or credit unions do not." Before the Honda case, regulators, including the DOJ and CFPB, had already pursued similar lending discrimination claims based on race against automobile dealers including a case resulting in a $98 million settlement by Ally Financial which did not take applications directly from consumers and instead made most of its loans through car dealers nationwide who were allowed to add discriminatory markups based on race. There are other studies after the Ayers studies that further demonstrate the existence of unique consequences for blacks while negotiating. One study suggested that "real estate agents have been found to more frequently offer to white [rather] than minority homebuyers 'reduced closing costs or lower mortgage rates through affiliated lending and service companies.' "

Ian Ayres has even more recently noted, in a 2011 unpublished paper with co-authors Mahzarin R. Banaji and Christine Jolls, that more nuanced and technical forms of negotiating such as through electronic bartering and auction services like eBay have also indicated biased results for black persons. Ayres and his co-authors constructed a field experiment to test the effects of race on transactions involving baseball card auctions on eBay. The tester elements involved a display of photographs showing the cards being "held by either a dark-skinned/African American hand or a light-skinned Caucasian hand." Their results indicated that the "[c]ards held by African-American sellers sold for approximately 20% ($0.90) less than the cards held by Caucasian sellers."

> **Negotiation Nugget**
>
> For more information on the eBay experiment, see Ian Ayres et al., *Race Effects on eBay*, 4 Rand. J. Econ. 891 (2015).

A similar study on the effects of race in negotiations was also created by Jennifer Doleac and Luke Stein in the on-line sale of an Apple iPod. These researchers "posted classified advertisements offering an iPod Nano portable digital music player for sale on several hundred locally focused websites throughout the US" and signaled race by the skin color of the hand holding a picture of the iPod being offered for sale in the advertisement. This study differed somewhat from the Ayres eBay study because the eBay parties would never expect to meet and the purchases through eBay were insured by eBay. The participants in the iPod study would expect to meet in person to close the deal, and there was no insurance involved.

The Doleac and Stein study specifically used pictures of a man's black hand, or a man's white hand, or a man's white hand with a tattoo, each holding a new, unopened iPod Nano. Potential buyers responded via anonymized email addresses. There was no formal bidding process and "either party [could] cease communication at any time without facing any consequences." About two hours after each advertisement was posted, the researchers sent an email to each responder stating they received numerous responses and asked for their best offer. From these results, the researchers concluded: "Black sellers receive 18% fewer offers than white sellers, whereas tattooed sellers receive 16% fewer." Also, with respect to amounts, the mean offer received was $49.86 and maximum offer of $54.05. But, "[c]ompared with white sellers, black sellers receive average offers of $5.72 (11%) lower and tattooed sellers $5.53 (10%) lower." Further, the researchers concluded that both "[b]lack and tattooed sellers" received the "best offers" which were "also lower than whites', by $7.07 (12%) and $6.60 (11%), respectively."

Final conclusions from Doleac and Stein were that "black sellers suffer worse market outcomes than their white counterparts" including the receipt of "13% fewer responses and 18% fewer offers" and these negative results were "similar in magnitude to those associated with a seller's display of a wrist tattoo." Also, this study found that "black sellers do better in markets with larger black populations, suggesting that the disparities may be driven, in part, by buyers' preference for their own-race sellers."

* * *

[O]ne can see how a black person might have realistic expectations that actual negotiations will result in nothing but poor results—based on being black. And black persons, more likely than any other racial group, tend to find themselves pressured to "cover" or conform to norms that deny their racial identity at work. This form of covering in salary negotiations represents a tradeoff between the lesser of two evils related to racial stereotyping[.] She must act against her own financial interest to lose the battle for a higher negotiated salary in order to win the war of not losing out on overall professional opportunities for being viewed as incompetent or unqualified or lazy based upon a racial stereotype.

* * *

As a result, and beyond attempting to capture much of the literature identifying harsh consequences when negotiating while black, this chapter should highlight one final concern. Unless the black person in the negotiation has as much information as a similar white counterpart, be it through social or Internet networks or some other means, and the white person negotiating with her focuses on excising any conscious and subconscious race-based stereotypes from the process, negotiating while black, even in 2015 and even with relatively well-meaning counterparts, means that unproductive obstacles still exist. . . .

POINTS FOR DISCUSSION

1.   What is someone to do when faced with such significant and abhorrent behavior? Negotiation expert Marty Latz offers this advice: find common interests to build rapport, focus on objective standards, and decide offer-concession moves based on patterns. Building rapport, he explains, is an attempt to redefine the "in-

group" away from race and toward a commonality to minimize unconscious bias. Focusing the negotiation on objective standards—a fundamental negotiation concept we discuss in Chapter 2—sets the value of the negotiation on factors neither side controls thereby minimizing the extent that race is a factor. Following offer-concession patterns, simply described as modeling your strategy after what either works or is expected in the particular setting, requires deep knowledge of one's negotiation environment. What all of these strategies require, however, is preparation. Marty Latz, *Power Strategies to Counter Racial Discrimination in Negotiations* (available at https://www.expertnegotiator.com/tip/counter-racial-discrimination-in-negotiations/?utm_source=monthly%20column&utm_medium=email&utm_campaign=monthly%20column).

2.   As with his comparison of gender in his negotiation class, Professor Craver has examined the results of negotiation assignments with law students for effects of race.

> In my study, I compared the negotiation results achieved over a nine-year period by Black and White students in my Legal Negotiation class. I did not find a statistically significant difference for a single year or from the combined data. These results strongly suggest that the participant's race does not affect negotiator performance.

Charles B. Craver, *What Makes a Great Legal Negotiator?*, 56 Loy. L. Rev. 337, 342 (2010). Is this somewhat of a rebuttal of the studies' findings, or is something else going on? Note that the participants in the Craver study were all law students who chose to take Professor Craver's negotiation course, not a random sampling of the general public. Do you think law students' reactions to race are different than those of the general public?

3.   Several noted scholars have expressed concerns about how less powerful parties or members of disadvantaged groups are likely to fare in consensual dispute resolution processes like negotiation or mediation. See, e.g., Richard Delgado, Chris Dunn, Pamela Brown, Helena Lee & David Hubbert, *Fairness and Formality: Minimizing the Risk of Prejudice in Alternative Dispute Resolution*, 1985 Wisc. L. Rev. 1359; Trina Grillo, *The Mediation Alternative: Process Dangers for Women*, 100 Yale L.J. 1545 (1991). Professor Delagado recently revisited these themes arguing that despite the near ubiquity of informal dispute processing, such procedures still disadvantages poor and historically disadvantaged communities. Richard Delgado, *Alternative Dispute Resolution: A Critical Reconsideration*, 70 SMU L. Rev. 595 (2017). Richard Delgado, *The Unbearable Lightness of Alternative Dispute Resolution: Critical Thoughts on Fairness and Formality*, 70 SMU L. Rev. 611 (2017). Does the Green excerpt corroborate their concerns?

4.   In the early 1990s researchers looked at both litigated and mediated outcomes for minorities in the small claims court in Bernalillo County Metropolitan Court in Albuquerque, New Mexico. The study found that minority claimants

consistently received less money in mediation than non-minorities, while minority respondents consistently paid more. Despite these results, minority claimants were more likely than non-minority claimants to express satisfaction with the mediation process. Why do you think this is the case? See Michele Herman, Gary LaFree, Christine Rack, Mary Beth West, METROCOURT PROJECT FINAL REPORT: A STUDY OF THE EFFECTS OF ETHNICITY AND GENDER IN MEDIATED AND ADJUDICATED SMALL CLAIM CASES (1993). Following up on the claim that dispute resolution processes produce biased outcomes based on gender, race, ethnicity, or socio-economic status, Gilat J. Bachar and Professor Deborah R. Hensler identified 38 studies where this hypothesis was tested. Due to the contrary and inclusive results, they concluded that the answer is "we don't know." Gilat J. Bachar and Deborah R. Hensler, *Does Alternative Dispute Resolution Facilitate Prejudice and Bias? We Still Don't Know*, 70 SMU L. Rev. 817 (2017).

5.   Professor Alyson Carrel argues the negative impact of private settlement on disadvantaged groups may abate through the adoption of a cybersecurity platform called Multi-Party Computation, in which private settlement data can be encrypted and computed to provide anonymized and aggregated data about the extent to which certain harms are taking place in society. Alyson Carrel, *Reimagining Settlement with Multiparty Computation*, NW. J. Tech & Intell. Prop BLOG (May 19, 2020), https://jtip.law.northwestern.edu/2020/05/19/reimagining-settlement-with-multi-party-computation/.

CHAPTER 7

TECHNOLOGY AND INNOVATION

If technology-related change has so deeply affected so many practices in our professional and personal lives, it would stand to reason that it applies, in some way, to negotiation as well. That negotiation is a human constant, a fundamental frame of human interaction, might be true—but only in the most general sense. "People have always negotiated, and probably will always negotiate, with each other in their personal and professional lives" is probably a valid statement, at least to the extent that we can recreate human interactions in the past and forecast their interactions in the future. However, this does not equate with saying "people have always negotiated in the same way, in the same contexts, with the same understanding of the interaction, with the same perception of the other and with the same attitude toward their own goals." Acknowledging negotiation as a constant interactional framework is one thing; assuming that the how, why, where, what and when of negotiation are *all* human constants is quite another.

Noam Ebner, *Negotiation is Changing*, 2017 J. Disp. Resol. 99, 106 (2017) (emphasis in original).

In this chapter, we explore how technology and innovation are shaping negotiation in the 21st-century. More specifically, we focus on how technology has increased options for where and when to communicate and has allowed us to gather and harness data to support decision-making. Within those lenses, we revisit earlier concepts such as cultural competency, trust, cognitive biases, communication, and BATNA through the lens of technology.

A. TECHNOLOGY AS COMMUNICATION CONDUIT

In the wake of the COVID-19 pandemic, technology became a vital, if not sole, means of communication for many. After years of skepticism and concern about the use of technology in the legal and dispute resolution professions, lawyers were forced to quickly adopt and adapt to technology to continue providing effective legal services.

While the daily average number of users increased 300% on the video conference platform Zoom, there are many other technology platforms from which to choose when negotiating: telephone, email, and in platform chats/direct messages/instant messages. Each communication platform presents unique benefits and risks. Negotiators must assess and analyze which communication mode is best suited for their situation just like they would analyze their client's interests or BATNA.

When selecting the most appropriate mode of communication, consider the following two variables: *where* (in-person or in text-based and video-based platforms) and *when* (synchronously or asynchronously). Below, we have excerpted two articles that explore these variables. The first article focuses on negotiating via email: an asynchronous text-based platform. The second article focuses on negotiation via video conferencing: a synchronous video-based platform.

1.   Negotiating Via Email

NOAM EBNER, NEGOTIATING VIA EMAIL
in 1 THE NEGOTIATOR'S DESK REFERENCE 116, 119–129
(Andrea Kupfer Schneider & Christopher Honeyman eds., 2017)

* * *

Negotiating Through Email: Seven Major Challenges

We now move on to delineate seven areas in which interacting via email affects elements or dynamics of negotiation. . . . These areas are:

1.   More contentious, and less cooperative, process

2.   Fewer, or less, integrative outcomes

3.   Diminished trust

4.   Increased attribution and increased misinterpretation

5.   Diminished privacy

6.   Diminished negotiator focus

7.   Diminished negotiator commitment and investment

1.   More Contentious, and Less Cooperative, Process

In online communication, parties tend to be even less inhibited than in face-to-face communication, due to physical distance, reduced social presence, reduced accountability, and a sense of anonymity. The lack of social cues causes people to act more contentiously than they do in face-to-face encounters, resulting in more frequent occurrences of swearing, name calling, insults, and hostile behavior. E-negotiators are more likely to threaten and issue ultimatums; to lie or deceive; to confront each other negatively; and to engage in flaming.

Another media effect, deriving from email negotiation's lack of synchronicity, involves what Anne Marie Bülow has dubbed a "double monologue" style of interaction: parties cherry-pick pieces of the conversation that they wish to relate to, ignoring others; they relate to these issues in long, argumentative statements. One result is that communicating through email, negotiators tend to work simultaneously to persuade each other that they are right, rather than explore ways to work together. This precludes questioning, so less information is shared. It also precludes uptake . . . so information the other has shared might not be discussed, clarified and expanded. Finally, to the extent that queries are used, they tend to be short and specific—extracting specific information but not opening the door to other information. As a result, one might extract a factual detail from one's counterpart, but not the interest underlying it.

All the above can easily result in a lack of process cooperation, as parties focus on the person rather than on the problem, and as they do so, the potential for effective information-sharing decreases. Parties may not elicit, or may ignore, important information the other has conveyed, as well as relational cues. The use of email may, therefore, accentuate competitive behavior in negotiations. Not only do parties to email negotiation act uncooperatively—they feel justified in choosing this pattern of behavior. . . .

* * *

2.   Fewer, or Less, Integrative Outcomes

. . .[I]nformation shared in email negotiations is likely to be constrained, analytical, and contentious. Even if process cooperation devolves no further, this information is hard to work with, which might explain an email negotiator's reduced accuracy in judging the other party's interests. Such reduced accuracy would reduce negotiators' ability to accurately assess differential preferences and identify potential joint gains. . . .

Indeed, many experiments measuring these two elements—process cooperation and integrative outcomes—illustrate significant challenges. First, e-negotiation appears to entail lower rates of process cooperation, and lower rates of integrative outcomes, when compared to face-to-face negotiation. Second, in email negotiation the potential for impasse appears to be greater than in face-to-face negotiation. . . . Recent writing on this issue has suggested that negotiator orientation towards cooperation or competition determines whether the outcome will be integrative far more than the communication channel affects this issue. People with cooperative orientations will generally be able to convey and implement this despite any challenges that constraining communication channels pose to them.

* * *

3.   Diminished Degree of Inter-Party Trust

... Communicating via email, negotiators must cope with threats to trust that are inherent in the medium and in its use. Email negotiators trust their counterparts less than negotiators in similar face to-face interactions, at all stages of the process. Before the process's inception, e-negotiators report a comparatively low level of trust in their opposite. This low trust-level persists throughout the course of the negotiation, resulting in diminished process cooperation and information sharing. Even after reaching deals with their opposites, e-negotiators trust their opposites less than participants in face-to-face negotiations, manifesting in lower degrees of desire for future interaction with them. Why do people distrust each other online—or, more to the point, what is it they are worried about? It may be that they are specifically concerned about intentional deception. There is little research available on lying in e-negotiation, although it has been suggested that people may have more tendency to act deceptively when communicating through lean media. This gives cause for concern, given that we are considerably less skilled in intuitively detecting deception online than we are in face-to-face settings; while more deliberate methods for picking up on textual cues are being developed, a great deal of technical sophistication is required to successfully conduct such analysis in the course of a real-life-negotiation. To compound the issue further, research has shown that e-negotiators are more likely to suspect their opposite of lying, even when no actual deception has taken place. As negotiators, then, we are suspicious of our counterpart's honesty—but our suspicions rarely target the true liars out there. Given that in lean media we tend to react strongly in retaliation to perceived lying, we may damage a relationship irreparably over an erroneous judgment—or our counterpart may do so, over their judgment of our own veracity.

* * *

4.   Increased Attribution and Increased Misinterpretation

Communicating through lean media increases the tendency toward the fundamental attribution error: parties perceive negative actions or statements on their opposite's part and interpret these as outgrowth of the other's negative intentions and character—rather than as unintended results of circumstance. Reduced social presence and few contextual cues lend a sense of distance and vagueness to the interaction. People tend to overestimate the degree to which they communicate clearly over email. Subtle elements of communication, such as sarcasm or humor, are particularly vulnerable to such overconfidence. The media richness element of interactivity compounds this: E-negotiators ask fewer clarifying questions than face-to-face negotiators—leaving more room for assumptions to form and take root. Attribution dynamics will cause these assumptions to tend toward the negative. Analysis of failed email negotiations shows that they tend to include unclear messages, irrelevant points, and long general statements, each of which provides ample breeding ground for attribution.

* * *

5.   Diminished Privacy

Maintaining privacy in a negotiation process is never an easy task. In face-to-face negotiation, parties can, and do, share information about the negotiation with their friends, families and colleagues, and occasionally with wider circles. However, parties can, at least, meet in a private setting, close a door on the world, or lower their voices—eliminating real-time "sharing." In email negotiation, by contrast, you never know who is "in the room" with you. Your opposite may have showed your email to their boss, their colleagues or your competition, before responding to you. The messages you transmit are forever archived somewhere beyond your control. The information you share might reach people with whom you had no wish to share it. Your counterpart doesn't have to be malevolent in order for this to happen. It might be you who unintentionally clicks "reply all" instead of "reply," sending your private message into a public domain!

* * *

6.   Diminished Party Focus

Communicating via email, negotiators are likely to suffer media-related effects including confusion, low cognitive retention of previous messages, and diminished concentration. This is due to several factors, including time passage between information exchanges, the tendency to answer emails in spurts and sections rather than finding the time to write full messages, and the tendency to answer emails in less-than optimal surroundings and circumstances. In addition, email is often not something we train our full attention on, but rather something we do as part of our media multitasking. We check our email as we surf the web, and we surf the web as we read or reply to our email—perhaps holding in-person or phone conversations at the same time.

In general, research suggests that in the digital age, human attention span is decreasing. The explanation that we are now "multitasking" provides no relief, given the research indicating that we are not as good at multitasking as some of us like to think we are. Heavy multitaskers suffer a range of shortcomings as opposed to "focusers," many of which are pertinent to negotiation: they are not good at filtering out irrelevant information, and are easily distracted. They tend to have low detail recall, and despite their tendency to switch between tasks rapidly, they are not skilled at this, as their brain is always somewhat focused on the task they are not doing. Negotiators suffering from any of these, due to their multitasking tendency, work surroundings, or email-management habits, might be confused and unfocused. So, too, might be negotiators communicating via smartphone in noisy or crowded environments without taking care to consider the effects their surroundings may have on their capacity to focus. In particular, the multi-screen environment presented by many home, work, and entertainment venues primes our brains to latch onto new stimuli. Negotiators who multitask while they are negotiating, in the form of reading messages on a smartphone while negotiating face-to-face, have been found to achieve lower outcomes. Without social norms holding us back from reading that message that just came in, we are much more likely to allow ourselves to let attention slip in this way.

* * *

7.   Diminished Party Commitment and Investment

Parties to email negotiation might be less motivated than face-to-face negotiators. They have not displayed the minimum commitment of getting up, getting dressed and coming to the table; indeed, they might not have any sunk costs at all. Smartphones have compounded this issue by reducing even the value of the time invested in writing the email; people can now do this during low-value time—while commuting, waiting for someone to show up, during lunch, etc. Email allows people to easily initiate low-investment "shot in the dark" approaches. This might partially explain reports of higher impasse rates in email negotiation, as well as the phenomenon of email negotiations evaporating, with one party simply dropping out of the conversation.

1.   Professor Ebner points to seven areas in which email negatively impacts negotiation dynamics. Can you describe how a few of these areas might create opportunities?

2.   Professor Ebner describes email as a "constrained, analytical, and contentious" form of communication. Newer platforms, such as Slack and Microsoft Teams, create a more synchronous feel to text-based communication and use short and informal messaging. Do you think this counteracts the diminishment of interparty cooperation aspect of email?

3.   In Chapter 6, Professor Michael Green explored the role of Internet platforms in creating the ability to gather and exchange information without sharing or disclosing information about one's demographics. Michael Green, *Negotiating While Black*, in THE NEGOTIATOR'S DESK REFERENCE (Andrea Kupfer Schneider & Christopher Honeyman eds., 2017). How might individuals use technology facilitated communication to combat biases? How might these platforms encourage marginalized or perceived lower-status individuals to participate more? Increasingly, email platforms and apps include profile pictures, names, and associated positions or titles. How might these newer features reintroduce social context cues leading to implicit bias?

4.   Professor Ebner discusses the increased multitasking that stems from the ubiquitous use and access of email on smartphones. Professor Lauren Newell points to research demonstrating that the digital generation, individuals who grew up using technology on a regular basis, has lower attention control than older generations and recommends lawyers take technology breaks and practice meditation to overcome this. Lauren A. Newell, *Reclaiming Attention in the Digital Generation Negotiator*, in 1 THE NEGOTIATOR'S DESK REFERENCE 201 (Andrea Kupfer Schneider & Christopher Honeyman eds., 2017). How might you counteract this decrease in party focus?

5.   To what extent might generational differences among the negotiators amplify or diminish the challenges and opportunities identified by the authors? Nikola Simkova and Zdenek Smutny argue that companies should choose a mode of communication for business-to-business negotiations based on who is negotiating. They found that millennials prefer computer-assisted platforms. Nikola Simkova & Zdenek Smutny, *Comparison of Unassisted and Smart Assisted Negotiation*, in B2B RELATIONSHIPS FROM THE PERSPECTIVE OF GENERATION Y, 10 Info. 263 (2019).

2.   Negotiating Via Video Conference

Many people mistakenly believe that video conferencing solves the complications of email because, unlike email, it is a synchronous mode of communication. In the following excerpt, however, Professor Noam Ebner describes a number of issues that arise for negotiations conducted via videoconference. Below he identifies three trust-related challenges that videoconferencing might pose to a negotiator.

NOAM EBNER, NEGOTIATION VIA VIDEOCONFERENCING
in THE NEGOTIATOR'S DESK REFERENCE, 155, 164–66
(Andrea Kupfer Schneider & Christopher Honeyman eds., 2017)

* * *

Video restores "otherness": Video reintroduces issues into the negotiation process, whose effects were diminished by text-based communication: race, gender, stereotypes and more. The salience of these elements is heightened once again by parties' visual availability to one another. Some of their effects include challenges to trust—ranging from the challenge of creating quick identification-based trust with a

> **Negotiation Nugget**
>
> For six tips on effectively negotiating via videoconference platforms, see https://youtube/mi1uOo5QAKg

counterpart who is very different from you in appearance to the bigger-picture dynamics of in-group/out-group stereotyping. In videoconferencing, these issues may turn out to be even more salient than in face-to-face settings! The side-by-side portrayal of both participants' videostreams in videoconferencing settings results in both of them being highly visible to each other concurrently, whereas in face-to-face settings, you see the other— but, for the most part, you do not look at yourself. This may serve to bring differences to the forefront of the subconscious identification process.

* * *

Technology and trust: At the time of writing, technological mishaps remain fairly common in videoconferencing. Screens freeze, video or audio

> **Note**
>
> Three kinds of trust are defined in Chapter 2 Section E: calculus-based trust, knowledge-based trust, and identity-based trust.

sometimes cut out, audio/video lag occurs, and more. Technological mishaps often have trust-related effects. . . . [Y]ou might begin to feel annoyed by [a counterpart complaining they can't hear you]. After all, your equipment and surroundings are all fine; there's something going on, on your counterpart's side. Why can't your counterpart buy a better phone? Why can't they stay put in a place with good cell reception, instead of moving around all the time? Are they showing you a lack of respect, by doing other things as you converse? Might they be doing this on purpose, to throw you off your game? Either way, they are being unprofessional and perhaps contentious. Should you really roll the dice on reaching a deal and working with them?

... When this occurs, judgmental biases such as the false attribution error are quick to kick in—and these can easily undermine trust.

* * *

I trust you as far as I can see you: In videoconferencing-based negotiation, we can see our counterpart; however, our view is limited to a very particular box, and from a single perspective. Quite naturally, we wonder what is going on *outside* of that box. Is something else attracting our counterpart's attention? Is the entire setting congruent with what we see, or might our counterpart be putting on a show? Is there anyone else in the room, listening in, without our counterpart letting us know?

These lines of thought are often triggered by other issues . . .—such as technical limitations and misinterpretation of body language. . . . [T]hese thoughts often take on the flavor of *suspicion*, an initial level of distrust. Suspicion presents a fertile breeding ground for false attribution error—with its detrimental effects on trust.

> **Negotiation Nugget**
>
> In the Netflix series, Tiger King, two parties are on the telephone with a mediator where, unbeknownst to the mediator (or opposing party), an unidentified individual is covertly listening in on the phone call and interrupts the discussion. This breach of trust and confidentiality immediately ended the call and any chance of resolving the dispute. *See* https://www.mediate.com/articles/fisher-mediation-tiger-king.cfm.

POINTS FOR DISCUSSION

1.   In the above excerpt, Professor Ebner argues that trust between negotiators is negatively impacted when there are "technology mishaps." He writes, "While there is no sure-fire way around these challenges, you can preempt technical mishaps proactively; in fact, take leadership in this area. In a study on online

mediators, mediators' expertise with the medium, and ability to troubleshoot, were found to be trust-generating in parties; a similarly positive effect might occur in negotiation. Take the time to familiarize yourself with the ins-and-outs of a platform, so you can guide others experiencing trouble. Another way to demonstrate leadership and savvy as well as pre-empting some of the attribution effects discussed above, is by recommending that you decide ahead of time on a backup communication channel—a different videoconferencing platform, or a phone call conversation." Noam Ebner, Negotiation via Videoconferencing, in 1 The NEGOTIATOR'S DESK REFERENCE 165 (Chris Honeyman & Andrea Kupfer Schneider eds., 2017).

Negotiation Nugget

For an updated list of states that have adopted the technology competency duty, see LawSite Tech https://www.lawsitesblog.com/tech-competence.

2. While it is prudent to familiarize yourself with the technology platforms before a negotiation, it may also be ethically required. According to MRPC Rule 1.1, Comment 8, lawyers must demonstrate competence by not only staying abreast of changes in the law, but by understanding the risks and benefits of associated technology as well.

3. How might technologies used as a communication intermediary provide better client protection in lawyer-as-settlor situations? The increasing use of technology as a means of negotiating online presents interesting opportunities for greater scrutiny and regulation.

4. The use of technology as a communication conduit is sometimes referred to as the "fourth party," a term coined by Ethan Katsh and Janet Rifkin to describe the impact technology has on the facilitation of dispute resolution processes such as mediation where a third-party neutral normally facilitates the communication among disputing parties. Orna Rabinovich-Einy and Ethan Katsh describe different examples where technology increasingly plays a role as a fourth party to facilitate the negotiation beyond simply serving as a conduit for communication.

> The introduction of technology into the design of the process in the form of the technological 'fourth party' has both generated completely new types of processes unimaginable in the face-to-face era and separated some familiar dispute resolution processes from qualities and traits previously considered significant, if not essential, to their design and operation. A clear example of a new process is the emergence of automated and technology-assisted negotiation/mediation approaches, which include problem identification processes (eBay), mechanisms for matching problems and solutions (SquareTrade), automated negotiation support systems (SmartSettle) and blind bidding tools (CyberSettle). These processes escape previously accepted clear-cut distinctions between direct negotiation and third-party dispute resolution, giving rise

to another sui generis category in which the 'fourth party' displaces the third party. These applications have been employed mainly in relatively simple disputes but can be expected to evolve and play a useful role and be a force for change in the managing of highly complex disputes.

Orna Rabinovich-Einy & Ethan Katsh, *Digital Justice: Reshaping Boundaries in an Online Dispute Resolution Environment*, 1 Int'l J. of Online Disp. Resol. 5, 32 (2014).

B. TECHNOLOGY AND DATA-DRIVEN DECISION-MAKING

In 2019, Professors Noam Ebner and Alyson Carrel implored the dispute resolution field to broaden their understanding of technology and explore the myriad ways in which technology can enhance, supplement, and assist mediators beyond simply serving as a conduit for communication. Alyson Carrel & Noam Ebner, *Mind the Gap*, 2019 J. Disp. Resol. 1, 1 (2019). Negotiators, too, should broaden their understanding and use of technology. Technology can provide a major assist to negotiation by facilitating data collection and analysis to inform decision-making processes. Because big data is increasingly informing decision-making in other professions, Ed Walters argues that lawyers may soon find they have a duty to utilize data when advising clients about litigation and settlement options. He writes:

> **Negotiation Nugget**
>
> Professor Carrel describes a myriad of ways in which technology such as litigation analytics and multi-party secure computation can innovate negotiation, see https://www.youtube.com/watch?v=6BTG 4U16ZI4.

Law firms are looking at litigation analytics more than ever to analyze the merits of arguments and litigation strategies—in no small part because the tools of analysis are improving quickly. For example: Tools from the recently launched Lexis Analytics and from Docket Alarm give a deeper look than ever at the strategies, judges, and law firms that help firms to understand litigation outcomes. . . . Clients need better information to make strategic decisions about litigation, and they are becoming increasingly sophisticated about pricing risk. In addition, litigation financing companies will have hundreds of millions of dollars at stake, so they will demand that firms are using analytics to understand the risks at trial. In addition to these gains, lawyers have an increasing capacity to understand how individual judges are likely to rule in a case or whether certain motions are likely to be granted. Today these tools are mostly descriptive; that is, they explain what has happened in similar cases in the past. Future tools will be more predictive, describing what is likely to happen in a particular case in the future. Lawyers have new probabilistic tools to analyze whether their clients are likely to prevail at trial, but the rules do not give clear guidance about how they should use them and what should be considered frivolous under the Model Rules. When a lawyer receives a settlement offer that is in the ninety-first percentile of settlements in similar cases, does she have an obligation to recommend settlement to a client? What if the chances of winning at trial are 26%? Does that increase the obligation to settle a case?

Digging Deeper

Ed Walters poses the question, "In a world of data analytics . . ., will it be malpractice to take to trial a case, in the presence of a settlement offer, if you can know from the data that the settlement offer is 40% higher than . . . the mean or median of settlements accepted in similar cases?" He explores this question in the video posted here: https://vimeo.com/279258224.

Ed Walters, *The Model Rules of Autonomous Conduct: Ethical Responsibilities of Lawyers and Artificial Intelligence*, 35 GA. ST. U. L. REV. 1073, 1083–84 (2019). In this section, we explore the use of data-analytics and algorithms by sharing the following excerpt in which Professor Jean Sternlight identifies the pros and cons of using data analytics to make negotiation decisions.

JEAN R. STERNLIGHT, *POURING A LITTLE PSYCHOLOGICAL COLD WATER ON ONLINE DISPUTE RESOLUTION*

2020 J. Disp. Resol. 1, 24–26 (2020)

* * *

[T]he psychology of judgment and decision-making reveals that computers have potential strengths in aiding disputants to reach negotiated solutions. First, to the extent disputants could benefit from being provided with more and better data, computers can be quite helpful. Computers are adept at both collecting and distributing data that can potentially help disputants see that they are being impacted by . . . various biases and heuristics . . . . For example, one reason disputes can be difficult to resolve is that both sides may be overly optimistic as to their chance of success in court and thus unwilling to compromise in a settlement. A computer could potentially present data to both sides regarding jury verdicts or settlements in comparable cases, and thus bring parties closer to resolution. Second, a computer could help disputants evaluate their options more rationally, moving them away from overreliance on emotion, sunk costs, anchoring, or miscalculations as to the value of future benefit or costs. . . .

Computers can also potentially help disputants reject "bad" settlements that do not serve their best interests. Sometimes, rather than block a "rational" settlement that some might say ought to occur, our human decision making and judgment heuristics may cause us to enter agreements we should reject. For example, our over-optimism, our fears, our desire to be liked, or our liking of others may cause us to accept settlement proposals that are not helpful. Computers, by presenting data, could potentially save disputants from this fate by helping them resist proposed settlements that do not serve their interests.

However, while it seems clear that computers and [Online Dispute Resolution]can potentially help in all the ways outlined above, I also believe that humans may often be better than computers at helping fellow humans deal with judgment and decision-making issues in negotiations. The mere provision of data will often fail to change peoples' minds precisely because human brains do not process data as a computer would. Rather, people are very skilled at interpreting new data in the way most favorable to them. So, even if a computer provides data on average settlements or jury verdicts, a plaintiff might tell herself that her broken leg was worse than the average broken leg, that she is more likeable than most plaintiffs, that defendant is less likeable than most defendants, and so on. Or, a defendant similarly may tell herself that the plaintiff's claim is weaker than the average claim. Also, if a disputant is impacted by such phenomena as anchoring, sunk costs, or framing, the mere presentation of data may not pull them away from their biased interpretation. Unlike computers, humans care how information is presented, and by whom.

Thus, it may well be that human mediators, lawyers, or friends are more effective than computers in helping humans deal with their emotions and other judgment and decision-making issues. It turns out that humans can be very talented at helping other humans make judgments and important decisions. For example, a human who is good at reflective listening can potentially defuse anger in a way a computer might not. Or, a human can help another human take a break or refocus or see that their tentative decision is fueled more by emotion than logic. A person (mediator or attorney or friend) who is trusted and perceived to be an expert can clearly and persuasively convey information or data to the disputants. If a trusted person conveys the very same information that the disputant might have gleaned from a computer, I believe the odds are greater that the information from the human source will better help dislodge a disputant from his or her unreasonable position.

Using their communication skills, people can listen to find out disputants' concerns. They can build rapport, not only through their words, but also by using body language and facial expressions. With the help of this rapport, they can build trust, and thus become quite influential. They can tell persuasive stories. They can use apt metaphors. In all of these ways and more, people can connect effectively with other people to help them make judgments and decisions. Just reading information in a chart, relevant though it may be, is not always going to be as useful as more human modes of interaction.

POINTS FOR DISCUSSION

1.   Professor Sternlight points to the importance of lawyers using skills such as "reflective listening" to help clients analyze the totality of the situation, instead of focusing exclusively on data, and recognize the emotions and cognitive biases that might impact their decision-making. What other negotiation skills might a lawyer use to help a client use data analytics most effectively?

2.   Professor Michael Moffitt, concerned that data analytics might create a false sense of certainty, argues a slightly different point. He says,

> A client who is told simply that his case is 'worth $1,500,000' has no sense of the shape of the distribution curve leading to this probabilistic conclusion, and even no sense of the likelihood of a $0 recovery or some other extreme outcome. A heavily quantitative approach risks inaccurately suggesting that financial payoffs are the only (or even most important) interest a client has, or should have, in deciding on a proper course of action. Virtually all clients have interests that extend beyond monetary terms. Even if it is possible to reduce nonmonetary interests into monetary valuations ('achieving certainty this year is worth $100,000 to me' or 'not setting a bad precedent is worth paying double on this

settlement'), the reduction to a single monetary term risks suggesting false or misleading equivalents for clients.

Michael Moffitt, *Settlement Malpractice*, 86 Univ. of Chicago L. Rev. 1825, 1863 (2019). What negotiation skills might a lawyer use in this situation to help a client use data analytics most effectively?

3. Although data analytics in the context of litigation and judicial decisions is growing in the United States, France made the controversial decision in 2019 to ban "judicial analytics" altogether. Violators may face up to five years in prison. Jason Tashea, *France Bans Publishing of Judicial Analytics and Prompts Criminal Penalty*, ABA Journal, June 7, 2019. How would one discover whether this prohibition has been violated?

4. Jena McGill and Amy Salyzyn argue that the increased use of data analytics in the law will benefit society by providing increased transparency into judicial behavior and decision-making. Jena McGill & Amy Salyzyn, Judging by Numbers: *How Will Judicial Analytics Impact the Justice System and Its Stakeholders?*, 44 Dal. L.J. (Forthcoming 2021).

5. Orna Rabinovich-Einy and Ethan Katsh detail the shift between private vs public resolution in three ways: 1) as parties move their private discussions online through a court ODR system, there can be no privacy expectations, 2) automated decision-making may limit human discretion in the resolution of disputes, creating a more rules-based system than traditional alternative dispute resolution, but raising concerns about fairness of automated processes, and 3) providing a data rich monitoring system of processes, neutrals, and dispute resolution systems design, but cautioning about the intrusion on privacy when doing so. Orna Rabinovich-Einy & Ethan Katsh, *A New Relationship between Public and Private Dispute Resolution: Lessons from Online Dispute Resolution*, 32 Ohio St. J. on Disp. Resol. 695 (2017).

> **Negotiation Nugget**
>
> ODR stands for the umbrella term "Online Dispute Resolution" which generally means the resolution of online disputes or the resolution of disputes in an online environment.

6. The use of analytics isn't without its complications. For example, biases can be baked into algorithms by humans training the systems and using data based on historical or social inequities. Professor Sternlight warns about the potential negative impact of using data analytics in the realm of adjudication and says,

Negotiation Nugget

Princeton Professor Ruja Benjamin explores biases in data science through the lens of human behavior, culture, and social justice, see https://youtu.be/rY8RkET3KC0.

[I]f the data made available to the computer is flawed or incomplete, or if the algorithm itself is biased, the computer's decisions will be faulty. Researchers have found that artificial intelligence can sometimes bake in biases we would prefer to eliminate. Therefore, it is quite conceivable that certain algorithmic forms of online dispute resolution could potentially be biased against classes of disputants on the basis of race, gender, ethnicity, age, or other factors.

Jean R. Sternlight, *Pouring a Little Psychological Cold Water on Online Dispute Resolution*, 2020 J. Disp. Resol. 1, 24 (2020). Professor Nancy Welsh sees similar issues in online dispute resolution.

Increasingly, courts, agencies, and repeat litigants (e.g., insurers, manufacturers, employers) are expressing interest in using ODR to resolve relatively routine, low-dollar disputes. ODR creates the opportunity for collecting and analyzing substantial amounts of data, which can then be used to detect problematic patterns. At the same time, the public is increasingly aware of the dangers presented by involvement with the online world, including the potential for security breaches, victimization as a result of inaccurate information, and unfairness as a result of biased algorithms. Consequently, many ODR advocates are calling for ODR procedures to be made transparent and accountable, with required reporting regarding the number of people using them, their substantive results, users' perceptions of the ODR process's fairness, demographic patterns, and the results of algorithmic audits.

Nancy Welsh, *Dispute Resolution Neutrals' Ethical Obligation to Support Measured Transparency*, 71 Okla. L. Rev. 823, 862–63 (2019).

7.   In Chapter 1, we talked about so many cases in litigation being settled through negotiation that it might be useful to consider them as one, in other words, "litigotiation." Could it be that we will focus more on comparisons to other negotiations and settlements than litigated outcomes? In Chapter 3, we discussed bargaining in the "shadow of the law." As more data is collected about the negotiation process through online dispute resolution platforms, how might this change the BATNA analysis?

INDEX

References are to Pages